Sacred Parenting

SACRED PARENTING

Jewish Wisdom for
Your Family's First Years

ELAINE ROSE GLICKMAN

URJ Press • New York

Every attempt has been made to obtain permission to reprint previously published material. The publisher gratefully acknowledges the following for permission to reprint previously published material:

CENTRAL CONFERENCE OF AMERICAN RABBIS: Excerpt from *On the Doorposts of Your House*, edited by Chaim Stern, Copyright © 1994 by Central Conference of American Rabbis. All rights reserved. Used by permission.

JEWISH LIGHTS PUBLISHING: Prayer for adoptive parents, in *Celebrating Your New Jewish Daughter: Creating Jewish Ways to Welcome Baby Girls into the Covenant — New and Traditional Ceremonies* © 2001 Debra Nussbaum Cohen (Woodstock, VT: Jewish Lights Publishing). Order by mail or call 800-962-4544 or on-line at www.jewishlights.com. Permission granted by Jewish Lights Publishing, P.O. Box 237, Woodstock, VT 05091.

THE JEWISH PUBLICATION SOCIETY: Excerpts from *The Jewish Study Bible, Tanakh Translation*. Psalm 20: For Difficult Moments, and Psalm 144: For Joyous Moments. Jewish Publication Society TANAKH translation copyright © 1985, 1999 by the Jewish Publication Society. Used with permission by The Jewish Publication Society.

Library of Congress Cataloging-in-Publication Data

Glickman, Elaine Rose.
  Sacred parenting : Jewish wisdom for your family's first years /
by Elaine Rose Glickman.—1st ed.
      p. cm.
Includes bibliographical references and index.
ISBN 978-0-8074-1089-9 (alk. paper)
  1. Parenting—Religious aspects—Judaism. 2. Child rearing—Religious aspects—Judaism.
3. Jewish religious education of children. I. Title.
BM725.4.G55 2009
296.7'4—dc22

2009012359

For permission to reprint, please contact URJ Press at:

URJ Press
633 Third Avenue
New York, NY 10017-6778

(212) 650-4120
press@urj.org

Printed on acid-free paper
Copyright © 2010 by URJ Press
Manufactured in the United States of America
10 9 8 7 6 5 4 3 2 1

For my mom and dad

Contents

Preface

You are blessed, Eternal One our God, Who makes me a mother in Israel.

I composed this prayer when my first child was only a few days old, that heady time of overpowering love, complete exhaustion, earnest befuddlement, and emotional peaks and valleys never experienced before or since. I remember whispering it into the darkness as I cradled him in my arms, nursing and rocking throughout the nighttime hours, and when I watched him sleep, his arms splayed out, the rise and fall of that little chest the most precious thing I had ever seen.

I have recited this prayer many times since, during the wonderful and terrible (mostly wonderful) days and nights of our three children's earliest years. I have recited it joyfully, when they rolled over from back to belly, at their first smiles and first steps, and standing silent next to their beds, filled again and again with dumbstruck love at the beauty of their sleeping forms. I have recited it to give me strength, during our little ones' battles with rotavirus and influenza, mysterious fevers that came and went, and the ear infections that were our son's constant companion during the first year of his life. And I have recited it not exactly ironically, rising at least five times a night to soothe a colicky infant, tearing the house apart looking for that other shoe (it was never found), when I slipped away for two minutes to use the bathroom (and maybe peek at an ancient issue of *People*) and returned to find all three children happily "making smoothies" in the kitchen, the floor covered in ice and water and mashed banana.

I like this prayer. I realize it doesn't hold a candle to the majesty of the *Sh'ma* or even the catchiness of "*Bim Bam*," but it's done a lot for me. It makes me remember I'm not alone; even when I've been the only adult caring for our children for going-on-seven hours, God is—somehow, somewhere—there with me. It also reminds me that our family unit is not alone; we are linked to a greater community, the entire people of Israel. And I like it because it acknowledges what is so easy to forget: that being a parent is a blessing. It's hard, and it's work, and it's sometimes soul-wringing, but it's a blessing. "You are blessed, Eternal One our God, Who makes me a parent in Israel."

I wrote this book for many of the same reasons I like this prayer. I wrote this book because parenting can be lonely, isolating; we may find it difficult to maintain old friendships or forge new ones, to adjust to a radically changed lifestyle, to hold onto the interests we used to cherish and even—it seems at times—the people we used to be. I wrote this book because when we go to stores or restaurants or especially board an airplane with little ones in tow, the looks we get are rarely of the "I'm so grateful to you for rearing the next generation" variety. I wrote this book because I really believe in the sacred importance of parenting, because I see it as holy work, and because I want to share the treasures of thousands of years of Jewish teaching and Jewish thought that can guide us along the way. And finally, I wrote this book because as a rabbi, a teacher, a writer, and a mother of three children, I think—and hope—that I have some practical wisdom to share as well.

❧

And yes, I've given my book the admittedly grandiose title *Sacred Parenting*. It sounds like such an exalted goal—and a goal that might appear so faraway, so unattainable. But it's actually closer than we realize—because sacred parenting is not the same as perfect parenting.

This statement might seem so obvious, but it came as a revelation—not to mention a relief—to me. For so long I felt that I had to do everything right in my parenting, had to anticipate every need and satisfy every want, had to fill every moment with smiles and sunshine, render every experience one of attachment and affection, project constant cheer and patience and serenity and joy. For so long I felt that was what it meant to parent—at least, what it meant to parent well.

But actually, that's what it means to parent with guilt, anxiety, and incredible stress. And somewhere along the line I realized sacred parenting trumps that type of parenting every time. Sacred parenting is not about doing everything just right, and it's not about beating ourselves up for being—well, ourselves. Rather, sacred parenting is about seeing ourselves and our children as cherished and loved and guided by a being far greater than ourselves, about letting God into our lives and our parenting, and about remembering that the work of parenting is holy and hallowed work. Sacred parenting is about doing the best we can, acknowledging our shortcomings and our disappointments but plowing ahead anyway, asking for the help we need; it's about finding meaning in the moment and savoring the sweetness of being a parent in Israel.

Rather than parenting with competitiveness, anxiety, and guilt, Judaism urges us to parent with spirituality, mindfulness, and partnership with God. I hope this book will help you parent in this way. I hope this book will help you engage in sacred parenting.

1

From Generation to Generation

*What the Bible and Our Ancient Rabbis Want Us
to Know About Being a Parent*

It is not in heaven, that you need say: "Who shall ascend for us to
the heavens, and bring it to us, and teach it to us, that we may do
it?" Nor is it beyond the ocean, that you need say: "Who shall cross
the ocean, and bring it to us, and teach it to us, that we may do it?"
But this thing is very near to you, upon your lips, and in your heart,
and you can do it.

—Deuteronomy 30:12–14

"**Y**ou can do it."

The Torah is pretty clear on this point. "You can do it." Maybe your
baby hasn't slept for more than three hours straight, waking up hysterical just as you manage to doze off. Maybe your toddler has just looked
you in the eye and shouted "No!" for the tenth time today—and it's only
9:45 in the morning. Maybe your preschooler has just finished coloring

a masterpiece—on your dining room walls. But even when you may not believe it, God believes in you. "You can do it."

And there are times you know it's true: "You can do it." It's three in the morning, you're snuggling your newborn in the rocking chair, and there is nowhere you would rather be. You're taking a walk with your little one and seeing the beauty of God's world through new eyes—through her eyes. You stub your toe, let out a yelp—then hear little feet running toward you and the sweetest voice in the world asking, "Are you okay?"

"You can do it."

This Deuteronomy quote has a trick up its sleeve, however. On one hand, it reminds us to believe in ourselves. To have confidence in what we can do. To take pride in what we are able to accomplish as we parent our children. But it does more than provide us with comfort. It provides us also with a charge.

The word that climaxes this passage—"*la'asoto*"—indeed means "you can do it." But it also translates to "you must do it."

"You must do it."

Parenting is important. It is essential enough to merit discussion in the Torah and the Bible, so vital that thousands of years ago, the greatest sages of Judaism devoted their attention to its challenges and its rewards. Parenting is something that must be done. And it must be done well.

We need both translations. "You can do it" encourages us. "You must do it" inspires us.

✥

Jewish tradition teaches that 613 mitzvot—commandments—are delineated in the Torah. The first of these is the mitzvah of becoming a parent.

On the sixth day of Creation, the Book of Genesis recounts, "God created humanity in God's own image; in the Divine image God created them. And God blessed them, and God said to them: 'Be fruitful and multiply, and replenish the earth.'"[1]

---

[1]Genesis 1:27–28.

"Be fruitful and multiply" means simply to become a parent—to bear a child, to adopt a child, to bring a child into a home and a family. In doing so, we "replenish the earth"—we ensure the survival of our species, our family, our community, our values. It is a sacred obligation—so sacred that the words *p'ru u'revu*, "be fruitful and multiply," were the first words God addressed to humanity. It is the first mitzvah; every other commandment flows from it.

❦

And in fulfilling the first commandment of the Torah—in becoming parents—we incur an entirely new and perhaps unfamiliar set of obligations. Author Roselyn Bell notes: "If *p'ru u'revu*—be fruitful and multiply—is the first dimension of Jewish parenting, *vesheenantam levanekha*—and you shall teach your child—is the second."[2]

What are we to teach, and how are we to teach it? How do we help the new lives God has entrusted to us grow into the people they must become?

We often hear what we might expect should be our primary concern for our children: "I just want my child to be happy." "I don't care what she does, as long as she's happy." "It's okay, look how happy she is." Happiness is indeed a Jewish value, so cherished that our matriarch Leah named a child in its honor![3] But Judaism teaches that happiness is more than self-indulgence, more than personal enjoyment, more than doing and having whatever we want whenever we want. Even when our babies are tiny, we know they need more than a simplistic definition of happiness. When we pick up crying infants and soothe them, we are not only making them happy—we are also teaching trust and compassion. When we change their dirty diapers, we are not only making our children happy—we are also teaching cleanliness and good health. When we baby-talk with our little ones, we are not only making them happy—we are also teaching communication and language. Even when we make our children laugh,

---

[2]Bell, 4.
[3]"Leah declared: 'What happiness!' So she named him Asher [literally, happiness]." Genesis 30:13.

we are not only making them happy—we are also teaching how to relate to the world and the people who surround them.

While we want our children to learn happiness, we hope that happiness will come from living well, and with meaning. As educator Jane Geller Epstein writes: "The goal [of rearing children] should be the creation of ethical, moral, mature, and self-confident human beings who are concerned about the lives and needs of others."[4] This description evokes children in whom any parent would take pride, the kind of people upon whom God's world depends. It also evokes an image that might seem light-years away from newborns still learning to roll over from tummy to back. Yet it helps us to see babies' early years not as discrete units—as simply "infancy" or "toddlerhood"—but as essential parts of their complete lives. It helps our children because so much of what they learn about the world—and so much of the people they will become—is rooted in these first years. And it helps us as parents because we are reminded that the hard work we put in with our babies—changing what seems like the thousandth diaper, reading board books when we might rather be reading the newspaper, rocking our children to sleep when all we want is to fall into bed ourselves, enduring tantrums and teaching limits—really does matter, and will matter for the rest of their lives.

Certainly Judaism emphasizes the centrality of the early years and the day-to-day work of childrearing. In fact, when our ancient Rabbis itemized parents' obligations to our children, their list consisted not of vague aspirations or far-reaching aims, but rather of concrete and specific responsibilities that begin almost as soon as babies are born. And while the responsibilities these Sages enumerated may seem foreign to us, we can actually find in them great—and timeless—wisdom.

According to the Talmud: "A father is obligated to circumcise a son, redeem him, teach him Torah, take a [spouse] for him, and teach him a

---

[4]Epstein, *The Jewish Working Parent,* 35.

trade. Some authorities say to teach him to swim, also... What is the reason? His life may depend on it."[5]

Let us take the liberty of reading "son" as "child," and of assigning these duties not solely to the father, but to either parent (or both parents). What, then, are the tasks with which we are charged? Circumcising and redeeming a child are two ancient institutions that welcome a son into the Jewish covenant; they parallel the *b'rit milah* (bris) ceremony for male infants and the festive naming celebrations for children of both genders. Teaching a child Torah ensures that she learns the ethical and ritual aspects of her heritage, and that she recognizes herself as part of a community. We might read "taking a spouse" as helping a child forge meaningful relationships, and "teaching a trade" as fostering her independence and self-sufficiency. Finally, teaching a child to swim—a necessary lesson in and of itself—refers also to giving the child the skills needed to grow up healthy and safe.

Much as we do, our ancient Sages envisioned children who would belong to a sacred community; practice ethical behavior and meaningful rituals; find a worthy life partner; and grow up skillful, independent, healthy, and safe. And as we do, our Sages understood that these hopes could be brought to fruition only through concrete, specific acts—through religious ceremonies, formal instruction, even swimming lessons. While our methods may differ in the modern day, we too fulfill concrete, specific duties for our children in order to help shape them into the people they can and should become.

※

But Judaism does not envisage the fulfillment of these duties as the sum total of parenting, our relationship to our children as governed entirely by a list of mandated tasks. From ancient to modern times, Jewish parents have sought to create cherished and loving bonds with our children, meeting our obligations to them in the context of a family life filled with happiness and mutual enjoyment.

---

[5]*Kiddushin* 29a, 30b, in Klagsbrun, 167.

As early as Abraham and Sarah, we find children welcomed and celebrated. Sarah greeted the news that she would become a mother with laughter,[6] and she and Abraham marked Isaac's weaning with Judaism's first party.[7] Leah was inspired to exalt God at the birth of her fourth son, naming him Judah—"I will praise the Eternal."[8] Our greatest Rabbinic leaders also took time to delight in their children. Rabbah bought toys for his little ones; knowing how much children love to break things, he chose already-damaged clay vessels that they could smash with impunity.[9] The esteemed Rabbi Joshua ben Levi once appeared at synagogue improperly attired, excusing his appearance by saying that he had been busy getting a child ready for school.[10] And colleagues seeking the wisdom of Rabbi Joshua ben Korhah once found the Sage at home crawling on all fours with a stick in his mouth, being led around by his small child.[11] Sages also skipped baths to hear their grandchildren recite Scripture;[12] postponed eating until their children had been taken to school;[13] planted trees in hopes their children would enjoy the fruits; offered special treats for snacks;[14] pondered how to keep little ones awake for a late-night dinner;[15] cut their studies short in order to prepare a child's meal;[16] and sat children on their laps for heart-to-heart talks.[17] The mother of Rabbi Joshua ben Hananiah even earned praise for bringing him to synagogue in a cradle during his infancy.[18] Amazingly, not only the care and love embodied in these activities, but also the activities themselves resonate with how we enjoy our own children today.

---

[6] Genesis 18:12.
[7] Genesis 21:8.
[8] Genesis 29:35.
[9] *Yoma* 78b, in Abrams, 152.
[10] *Kiddushin* 30a, in Abrams, 178–79.
[11] *Midrash Tehillim* 92:13, *Yalkut* Psalms 846, in Bialik 633:213.
[12] Jerusalem Talmud *Shabbat* 1:1, 3a, in Bialik 635:237.
[13] *Kiddushin* 30a, in Abrams, 178–79.
[14] *Shulchan Aruch*, in Wikler, 67.
[15] *Pesachim* 109a-b, in Abrams, 182.
[16] *Pesachim* 109a.
[17] *Bava Batra* 12b, in Abrams, 163.
[18] Jerusalem Talmud *Yevamot* 1:6, 3a, in Abrams, 177.

We may also find that ancient sentiments about parenting speak to the wonder, affection, and even exasperation we experience with our own children. Who but a parent could wryly observe that "when [parents] look upon their children, their joy makes them act like fools"?[19] Who but a parent could account for memory lapses or apparently diminished mental prowess by remarking that "children's chatter...removes a person from the world"?[20] And who but awestruck parents could apprehend God's miraculous design in creating from "a drop of fluid...completely perfected individuals"? [21]

✣

Tradition also places children at the center of Judaism's most sacred moments: the Exodus from Egypt, the Revelation of Torah at Mount Sinai, even the messianic redemption. Employing exalted images of children and familiar images of parenting, seers and sages rendered their visions of these events accessible and compelling.

No less a prophet than the great Isaiah draws on parenting motifs in his oracles. Evoking the triumph of salvation, Isaiah proclaims: "Thus says the Eternal God: Behold, I will lift up My hand to the nations...and they shall bring their sons in their bosoms, and their daughters shall be carried upon their shoulders. And kings shall be your foster-fathers, and their queens your nursing mothers...And I will save your children...And all flesh shall know that I the Eternal am your Savior, and your Redeemer, the Mighty One of Jacob."[22] Even more striking is Isaiah's use of a breastfeeding child to symbolize God's saving power: "You shall suck the milk of the nations, and shall suck the breast of kings; and you shall know that I the Eternal am your Savior, and I, the Mighty One of Jacob, your Redeemer."[23]

In their teachings and legends, our Sages, too, assigned children an essential role. According to one passage, infants led the Israelites in praising

---

[19]*Midrash Tehillim* 92:13; *Yalkut* Psalms 846, in Bialik 633:213.
[20]*Pirkei Avot* 3:14, in Abrams, 216.
[21]Leviticus *Rabbah* 14:2, in Abrams, 52.
[22]Isaiah 49:22–26, excerpted.
[23]Isaiah 60:16.

God after the splitting of the Red Sea: "Our Rabbis taught: Rabbi Yose HaGalillee expounded: At the time the Israelites ascended from the Red Sea, they desired to utter a song; and how did they render the song? The babe lay upon his mother's knee, and the suckling nursed at his mother's breast; when they beheld the *Shechinah* [God's presence], the babe raised his neck and the suckling released the nipple from his mouth, and they exclaimed, 'This is my God and I will praise God,'[24] as it is said, 'Out of the mouths of babes and sucklings have You established strength.'"[25] And at Mount Sinai, our Sages taught, the Israelites were not entrusted with Torah until they offered their children as guarantors:

> When the people of Israel stood at Mount Sinai ready to receive the Torah, God said to them, "Bring Me good securities to guarantee that you will keep it, and then I will give the Torah to you."
>
> They said, "Our ancestors will be our securities."
>
> Said God to them, "I have faults to find with your ancestors...But bring Me good securities and I will give it to you."
>
> They said, "Sovereign of the world, our prophets will be our securities."
>
> God replied, "I have faults to find with your prophets...Still, bring Me good securities and I will give the Torah to you."
>
> They said to God, "Our children will be our securities."
>
> And God replied, "Indeed, these are good securities. For their sake I will give you the Torah."[26]

Whether our Sages intended that these teachings be taken literally or metaphorically, the importance of children to the Jewish enterprise is clear and unmistakable. Children assume essential roles in the greatest episodes of Jewish history—the redemption from Egypt and the Revelation at Mount Sinai—and the greatest Jewish hope—a messianic era of universal goodness and peace. Perhaps inspired by passages such as these, Jewish folk wisdom teaches that with every child, the entire world begins anew.

---

[24] Exodus 15:3.
[25] *Sotah* 30b, in Abrams, 36–37.
[26] Song of Songs *Rabbah* 1.4, in Klagsbrun, 157.

Guided by a heritage that so celebrates children, Jewish parents are naturally inspired to place childrearing at the center of our lives. Ideally, we parent our children by treating them with the honor and respect befitting their unique and valued role in our tradition. Thinking of our children as the reason we merited the gift of Torah, as leaders in praising God at the Red Sea, and as an inspiration for some of our prophets' most resonant images surely reminds us of the esteem we owe our little ones.

But this is not the only truth Judaism offers. Here is another: While our children are God-given gifts worthy of our highest honor, they are also God-given responsibilities whom we must rear to become ethical, caring adults.

Although there are times—many, many times, we hope—to delight in, cater to, and celebrate our children, there are also times that we must love them enough to say no, to reprimand them, to set them on a different path. Judaism instructs us to value our children not only by exalting and acclaiming them, but also by instructing and guiding them.

Reminding us of this second aspect of childrearing, Jewish tradition parallels the list of parental obligations toward children with a set of children's obligations toward parents. So essential are these responsibilities that they are contained in two of the holiest sections of the holiest piece of Jewish literature—the Torah. In the Book of Exodus, God first charges us with the Fifth Commandment: "Honor your father and your mother, that your days may be long in the land which the Eternal your God gives you."[27] And Leviticus' Holiness Code includes God's words: "You shall be holy, for I the Eternal your God am holy. You shall revere—each of you—your mother and your father...I am the Eternal your God."[28] The placement of these decrees underscores their importance; according to the Talmud: "Our Sages taught: There are three partners in a person: the Holy One, a father, and a mother. When a child honors father and mother, the Holy One says: I account it as though they were honoring Me."[29]

---

[27]Exodus 20:12.
[28]Leviticus 19:2–3, excerpted.
[29]*Kiddushin* 30b, adapted, in Bialik 638:267.

As scholar Joseph Telushkin notes, it is "highly unusual to place respect for parents in a religion's most basic legal document."[30] Yet the Bible and Jewish law codes take pains to do exactly that. In fact, honoring one's parents is the first commandment for which the Mishnah promises eternal reward.[31] And the Talmud elaborates the specific ways in which children should fulfill the Torah's charge to "honor" and "revere" parents:

> Our Sages taught: What is 'reverence,' and what is 'honor'? 'Reverence' means that the son is not to stand in his father's place, nor to sit in his place; not to contradict him, nor to tip the scales against him. 'Honor' means that the son must supply his father with food and drink, provide him with clothes and footwear, and assist his coming in or going out of the house.[32]

Again we shall take the liberty of reading "son" as "child," and of ascribing these honors to either parent (or both parents). So how should children properly treat their parents? First with "reverence"—with formal expressions of respect that instill a sense of awe for one's mother and father. "Not [standing] nor [sitting] in a parent's place" means that if a mother or father has a customary chair, the child should not take it; although this might seem a minor issue, it is also a symbolic one, reminding the child of the parent's unique position in the family. "Not contradicting nor tipping the scales against [that is, siding in an argument]" a parent instills loyalty and respect for a parent's authority. Later additions to the Talmud's ruling include prohibitions against a child's waking her parents unnecessarily and calling parents by their first names.[33] Second, children are taught to treat parents with "honor"; according to the Talmud and subsequent commentaries, this means tending as much as possible to a parent's needs.

---

[30]Telushkin, *Jewish Humor,* 28.
[31]Mishnah *Pe'ah* 1.1.
[32]*Kiddushin* 31b.
[33]Levi, 35–36.

These tenets of childrearing might discomfit modern parents. Many parents today see ourselves not only—or even not primarily—as figures of authority in our children's lives. We also want to be our children's playmates, their confidantes, their loved ones. It is hard to imagine presenting ourselves as so exalted that our little ones dare not sit at our place at the breakfast table, so grand that our children must bring us food and drink—then scooping them into our arms, covering them with kisses, and taking them to the park.

Yet, while the specific duties outlined in the Talmud may appear archaic, they illuminate an essential aspect of parenting too often overlooked in modern society. There is—and there must be—a boundary between children and parents: the boundary of authority. Children must understand and accept parents' authority, and parents must take on this mantel of authority with confidence and assurance. For while we do want to have fun with our children, and inspire them to delight in us as much as we delight in them, our primary obligation is not to be our children's best friends or favorite companions. Our task, Judaism reminds us, is to be their parents—to nurture them, guide them, and help shape them into good, ethical, responsible, independent adults. And for us to accomplish this task, our children must not only like us and want to play with us, they must also revere and honor us.

At base, the Talmud's dicta are about instilling respect for authority—children's respect for their parents' authority, and parents' respect for their own authority. Although we will likely choose different ways to exemplify our authority than those outlined in the Talmud, we can still find both symbolic and concrete ways to demonstrate our position in the family. While we might allow our children to climb into our regular seat at the dinner table, we might also tell them that they may not play with Mommy's computer or sit at Daddy's desk. While we are likely to permit our little ones to disagree with us, we should ensure that they speak to us in a polite voice and accept our final decision. While we may let our children coax us out of bed when we would really rather sleep another hour, we might also teach them that there are certain times when—barring emergencies—Mommy or Daddy is not to be disturbed. While we may not mind our children's calling us or our friends by first names, we should be careful to teach respect for adults. And while we are perfectly capable of fetching our own apple from the kitchen or finding our own sweater, we might still encourage our little ones to assist us in household tasks appropriate to their age and ability.

By accepting the Jewish principle that we as parents are entitled to our children's reverence, and by teaching our children to feel and express this reverence, we are able to secure our parental authority. And ironically, once we feel confident in our authority, we may feel more relaxed and playful with our little ones. It is much easier and much more fun to take our children on outings, offer treats, or play silly games when we are certain that they will listen to us and respect the rules and limits we set. And our children, in turn, will ultimately feel more cared for, more trusting, and more self-assured knowing that they have parents who love them enough to be the boss.

While the idea of a toddler or preschooler taking on the formal obligations of honoring parents may appear ludicrous, we and our little ones actually benefit when we bear these ideals in mind from our children's earliest years. Indeed, the great Sages Rabbi Eliezer and Rabbi Joshua advised that it is easier to set children on the right path when they are still young; Rabbi Joshua even compared a small child to a wine branch, explaining: "[I]f you do not [shape] it when it is full of sap, once it hardens, you can do nothing with it."[34]

The Talmud illustrates this tenet when it poses the question of when a minor should be expected to fulfill the mitzvah of shaking the *lulav* on Sukkot. The Sages respond: "A minor who knows how to shake [the *lulav*] is subject to the obligation of the *lulav*; [if he knows how] to wrap himself [with the tallit] he is subject to the obligation...if he is able to speak, his [parent] must teach him...the *Sh'ma*."[35] From this discussion of Judaism's traditional ritual obligations, we can extrapolate a lesson on Judaism's moral obligations. If as soon as a child is able to shake the *lulav*, he is expected to shake the *lulav*, surely as soon as a child is able to begin expressing respect for his parents, he should be expected to do so. An eighteen-month-old, for example, can learn not to hit or bite his parents.

---

[34]*Midrash* Proverbs 22.6, Buber edition, 91, in Bialik 634:226.
[35]*Sukkah* 42b, excerpted, in Abrams, 156.

A two-year-old can use a nice voice to speak to Mommy and say please when asking for something from Daddy. A three-year-old can help with chores around the house, from setting out flatware to feeding the family pet. And by the age of four or five, a child can understand that certain places and privileges are reserved for adults. When these practices and attitudes are simply part of our children's reality from as early as they can remember, they grow up accustomed to respecting their parents and secure in their own cherished position within the family.

And Judaism teaches that in learning to honor their parents, children acquire another, even more important skill: learning to honor God, and the divine spark within themselves. The very structure of the Ten Commandments illustrates this lesson. The first four commandments—worshipping only one God, shunning idols and molten images, not taking God's name in vain, and keeping Shabbat holy—comprise humanity's obligations to God; the final five commandments—not murdering, committing adultery, stealing, bearing false witness, or coveting—comprise humanity's obligations to one another. In between these categories stands the Fifth Commandment, serving as a bridge between obligations human and Divine. Children who treat their parents—their nurturers and caregivers—with respect will come to treat God—our ultimate Nurturer and Caregiver—with respect as well; and children who see their revered parents nurturing and caring for them will see themselves as important people worthy of nurture and care. In revering and honoring parents, children come to revere God and honor themselves.

How, then, do we impart these behaviors to our children? How do we instill in them reverence, and how do we inspire them to demonstrate honor for us? We cannot simply demand that our children love and respect us, nor expect to foster these feelings in an atmosphere of unkindness or hostility. Rather, we teach our children love, honor, and respect by rearing them in an environment filled with love, honor, and respect.

A Chasidic story tells of a young boy whose parents were at their wits' end. The child was rude, disruptive, and unwilling to heed their demands for proper behavior. In despair, they brought him to the Rebbe, hoping for a miracle that might transform him into a loving, helpful child. After hearing their tale of woe, the Rebbe sent the parents away so that he might spend the day with the little boy. That evening, the mother and father returned to find their child affectionate, attentive, and respectful. They asked how the Rebbe had performed such a miracle with their incorrigible child; the Rebbe responded that all he had done was take the time to love the little boy, listen to him, and try to understand him.[36]

The Rebbe's gentleness and patience are echoed in other Jewish insights on childrearing. "Pleasant words are like honeycomb, sweet to the soul and health to the bones," teaches the Book of Proverbs,[37] suggesting that speaking kindly to our children strengthens them in both body and spirit. We are also reminded that we teach our children by example. If we expect our children to be truthful and reliable, Judaism charges us to be truthful and reliable ourselves: "A person should not promise to give a child something and then not give it," the Talmud warns, "because in that way the child learns to lie."[38] The Talmud further emphasizes the importance of loving attachments between parents and children, and a child's sense of being safe in her home. We are cautioned against "threatening a child even with a [small punishment]"[39] or "imposing an overpowering fear upon the household."[40] Finally, we must match our expectations to the ability of our children; parents are "forbidden to impose too heavy a yoke on [their] children...lest [parents] cause children to stumble."[41] In following these guidelines as we rear our children, we ensure that our children live in an environment of love, trustworthiness, attachment, and forgiveness; in such a home, they will naturally absorb these values and come to demonstrate them in interactions with parents and loved ones.

Jewish tradition is not, however, completely naïve. While over time most children will indeed learn and live out these values, coming to treat

---

[36]In Rosman, 21–22.
[37]Proverbs 16:24, in Radcliffe, *A Delicate Balance*, 25.
[38]*Sukkah* 46b, in Klagsbrun, 180.
[39]*Semachot* 2:5–6, in Telushkin, *Jewish Wisdom,* 155–56.
[40]*Gittin* 6b, 7a, in Telushkin, *Jewish Wisdom*, 155.
[41]*Shulchan Aruch, Yoreh Deah* 240:19, in Levi, 33.

with honor the parents who have honored them, there will be days—perhaps many—when things do not work out quite so neatly. Children try out many behaviors, testing parents to see precisely where the limits lie, proving to themselves that they are loved unconditionally, learning who exactly they are and who they want to be. While challenging, exhausting, and perhaps even infuriating, these milestones are also crucial as children develop from helpless newborns to curious infants, from striving toddlers to confident preschoolers. Coping with—and guiding our little ones through—these tumultuous times require more than the Rebbe's gentle and patient demeanor; after all, even the kindest voice and mildest expectations will not soothe an overtired two-year-old kicking and screaming in the candy aisle! Sometimes we must do more to elicit the behavior we expect from our children.

And indeed Judaism recognizes that certain times call for firm discipline, for punishment that children may not like but that ultimately proves beneficial. No less an authority than the Torah calls it a mitzvah— a sacred commandment—to rebuke a wrongdoer in the community;[42] how much more so are we obligated to rebuke our own beloved children when we see them straying from the right path! Failing to do so, our Sages caution, means nothing less than failing our children.

Rebuke is a fundamental aspect of good discipline and healthy families. Equally important, however, is that rebuke be given properly. While we may naturally feel frustration, impatience, and even anger when our children misbehave, we must remember that yelling at, berating, or physically or emotionally harming our children in the guise of "discipline" is not the Jewish way. Rather, we are guided to rebuke our children in private; to use a soft, pleasant voice; and to ensure that we do not bring undue shame to our little ones.[43] The celebrated Vilna Gaon added that parents reprimanding their children may not only mete out punishment; they must also clearly explain how to do the right thing in the future.[44] While these teachings may appear impossibly idealistic when we are actually faced with stubborn, willful misbehavior—and children who may

---

[42]Leviticus 19:17.

[43]Rambam, *Hilchot De'ot* 6:7, and Leviticus 19:17 with Rashi, in Radcliffe, *A Delicate Balance,* 74.

[44]In Saltsman, 179.

meet a soft, pleasant voice with a shrill, decidedly unpleasant "No!"—
they firmly remind us that punishment is intended never to harm or hu-
miliate, but only to ensure that our children will meet our expectations.

Perhaps the model of Jewish discipline is best illuminated in the Talmud's adage: "Always let the left hand thrust away, but the right hand
draw near."[45] While there will be times we must figuratively "thrust
away" our children—whether through verbal reprimands, time-outs, or
reasonable consequences—in order to discipline effectively, we do so only
with our left—the symbolically weaker—hand. With our right hand—
the symbolically stronger hand—we also reassure them of our love and
care, whether through affectionate words, special one-on-one time, or
simple hugs and kisses.

The Book of Proverbs teaches: "Train a child in the way he should go; and
even when he is old, he will not depart from it."[46] It is a deceptively simple
statement, revealing and summarizing so much about parenting Jewishly.
First, it reassures us; when we parent our children according to our beliefs
and values, we instill in them an ethos, a viewpoint, that will shape the way
they see the world and their place in it all of their lives. Next, it reminds us
how to achieve this sacred feat. We train our children; certainly we love and
celebrate our little ones, but we must also train them, teach them, discipline
them, guide them. And we do so "in the way [our children] should go"—
that is, to help our little ones reach their true potential, fulfill their unique
destiny, become the people they are meant to be.

As parents we are the custodians of our children, the caretakers of
their precious spirits, the divine spark God has implanted within them.
Our Sages marveled in the midrash: "Usually, if a man has given into
another's keeping an ounce of silver in private, and the latter returns to
him a pound of gold in public, the former will surely be grateful to the
latter. Even so it is with the Holy One, blessed be God. Humans entrust to
God a drop of fluid in privacy, and the Holy One, blessed be God, openly

<hr />

[45]*Sotah* 47a.
[46]Proverbs 22:6.

returns to them completely perfected individuals."[47] Developing from minute drops of sperm and egg, our children emerge as true miracles, true gifts from God. They are our children, to be sure; but they are also the ancestors of our descendants, and children of the living God. There is no worthier task than being our children's parents, of "guiding [our] sons and daughters in the right path," the midrash teaches, "'that [we] may know that [our] tent is in peace.'"[48]

Is any of this easy? Of course not. Jewish parents from ancient times to modern days have learned that rearing children can be as difficult as it is rewarding, as demanding as it is essential. Jewish legend teaches, in fact, that God warned the very first mother—Eve—that childrearing would "multiply thy trouble."[49] Yet for all of its challenges, it is something we would never give up. It is a primal, magnificent, and transcendent experience. It is a journey and a discovery. And perhaps it is easy to understand why it is also the first mitzvah—a sacred commandment given humanity on our first day of existence. It is something, after all, that must be done. And it must be done well.

The Torah tells us: "It is not in heaven, that you need say: 'Who shall ascend for us to the heavens, and bring it to us, and teach it to us, that we may do it?' Nor is it beyond the ocean, that you need say: 'Who shall cross the ocean, and bring it to us, and teach it to us, that we may do it?' But this thing is very near to you, upon your lips, and in your heart, and you can do it."

"You can do it." And "you must do it." Judaism charges us, but it also inspires us. We must do it. We can do it. Like a thousand generations before us, we are doing it. And for the thousand generations to follow, we will continue to do it well.

---

[47]Leviticus *Rabbah* 14:2, in Abrams, 52.
[48]*Yevamot* 62b, in Bialik 634:225.
[49]*Eruvin* 100b, in Bialik 633:214.

2

In the Beginning
A Welcome to Parenthood

Our world began with emptiness, Jewish tradition teaches. God dwelled in the midst of unfilled space, vast darkness, a deep and abiding void. God was alone. But out of this nothingness, God created the world. God created us. We became God's children. And God was alone no longer.

They are the first words of our Torah, and they are soul-stirring: "In the beginning God created the heavens and the earth."[1] In the beginning God took what was empty and filled it, with sea and sky, with sun and stars, with plants that bloomed and animals that swam and crawled and scuttled and stomped. All of these wonders, our ancient Rabbis marveled, were created for our sake. It was for us that God filled the emptiness. And we, in turn, filled the emptiness for God.

In the beginning God became our Parent, and we became God's children.

---

[1]Genesis 1:1.

In the beginning we become our children's parents. Out of emptiness we create a safe space for them, a place of care and compassion and unconditional—always unconditional—love. And in the beginning our children fill an emptiness in our lives we might not even have realized was there—a space that was created just for them, a place where they can grow and thrive and become the people God intends them to be.

It is the beginning. It is the beginning of a bewildering time, a soul-wrenching time, a crazy and overwhelming and impossible time. But more than that, it is the beginning of a wonderful time, a soul-exalting time, a crazy and beautiful and you-can-do-it time.

You are a parent. You are a family. And being a parent—creating a family—is the most important and most holy work you will ever do.

Mazal tov!

Be Fruitful and Multiply: Becoming a Family

It is the first mitzvah—commandment—in the Torah: "*P'ru ur'vu*," "Be fruitful and multiply."[2] And at first glance, it might appear to be one of the easiest commandments to fulfill. No need to eschew bread for a week during Passover, no mandate to procure a *lulav* and *etrog*, not even a warning to refrain from temptations like gossip and envy. "Be fruitful and multiply" means simply to become a parent.

Except that it is not so simple. The Mishnah records some of the earliest controversies:[3] Is this mitzvah incumbent upon men, or women, or both? How many children must we have to fulfill the commandment? Does the child's gender matter? What if we suffer a miscarriage, or divorce? The questions are at least two thousand years old. And they continue to this day.

Becoming a parent is not so easy. We struggle with infertility and treatments, surrogate parenthood and adoption. We suffer through nausea and sciatica, gestational diabetes and pregnancy-induced hypertension. We see specialists and genetic counselors, social workers and therapists.

---

[2]Genesis 1:28.
[3]*Y'vamot* 6:6.

We submit forms and personal statements, submit to background checks and home visits. We stay in the hospital for emergency fetal monitoring and to safeguard our own health, suddenly newly aware of the precarious process by which life comes into the world.

Each of our families is unique, and so is the journey each of us has made in becoming a parent. No journey is easy; some are more difficult—some much more difficult—than others.

Yet here we stand, having fulfilled this mitzvah—having become parents, and a family. Whether we birthed our children, adopted our children, or bore our children through surrogates does not matter. What matters is that we are parents. We have become families.

It seems completely amazing yet completely natural that this tiny child has become the new center of the universe. Phone calls go unreturned, mail goes uncollected, laundry goes unwashed, even clothes may go un-changed (hopefully this final phenomenon will not last long!). Every drop of energy focuses on baby: on changing diapers, tending to the stump of umbilical cord, figuring out the intricacies of breastfeeding and finding the best-flowing nipples for bottlefeeding, managing a warm sponge bath or two—not to mention all of the soothing, singing, swaying, and sim-ply staring with wonder at the beautiful creature who has—incredibly, magnificently—come into being.

According to Jewish teaching, a parent alone cannot claim credit for such a beautiful, breathtaking child. God is a partner in the child's cre-ation, too. Perhaps there is no clearer evidence of divine love than our miraculous children, and no more obvious reflection of divine goodness than their being entrusted to us. When we bask in the wonder of new parenthood, it is all the more special to imagine God's sharing in our joy and gladness as we contemplate our little ones.

And there are other times we need this teaching. There are other times we need to remember that God is with us in our parenting.

For there are times we may experience our new families not with un-diluted happiness but with confusion, fright, or anger.

If you are parenting with a partner, you may find that your spouse—whom you thought of as your other half, your beloved soul mate, the most cherished human being you will ever know—suddenly can't do anything right. He can't change a diaper; she can't get baby to stop crying. He won't throw in a load of wash; she won't stop nagging. She doesn't appreciate the work you do; he doesn't appreciate how overwhelmed you are. He isn't acting like the man you married; she isn't acting like the woman you fell in love with. If you are a single parent, you may feel isolated and unsupported, let down by friends and family whose assistance is not all that you had hoped. You may wonder anxiously how to go it alone, how to provide all that your child wants and needs, what will happen if you stumble along the way. You may grow fearful of the monumental and momentous tasks that stretch so far ahead.

And things with baby are not exactly rosy either. He will not stop crying, and you feel you've tried everything; she will not sleep, and you are more exhausted than you have ever been. She hasn't pooped in three days; he pees all over you every time you change his diaper. He develops jaundice; she develops a rash. She spits up after every feeding, and you wonder how much spit-up is normal and how much might signal reflux; he refuses to sleep unless he is in your arms, and you wonder how much of your impatience is normal and how much might signal that this is more than you can handle.

God is with us in these hours as well. We are not alone. Our babies are not alone, and our families are not alone. In our darkest and most difficult moments, we can reach out to God. We can whisper our frustrations to God as we settle into the rocking chair for the fifth time in a single night. We can murmur our fears to God as we contemplate how hard it has become to communicate with our loved ones the way we used to. We can ask God to strengthen and comfort us when we are not certain we'll make it through another minute, let alone the next eighteen years.

It can feel strange to talk to God at times like these. It can, however, grow to feel quite wonderful, too. It feels wonderful to have someone (Someone with a capital S, actually!) to confide in, Someone to Whom we can confess our deepest feelings and fears, Someone Who—in a case of happy irony—considers no hour too ungodly for listening. And over time, we may come to hear God answering us as well.

In the Book of Kings, the great prophet Elijah—pursued by an idolatrous queen—finds refuge in a mountaintop cave and seeks God's presence. Whirlwinds, great tremors, and fire pass before him—but God is not to be found. Only "after the fire, [in] a still small voice" does God make the Divine Presence known to Elijah.[4] These early days with baby—filled with night wakings and unbelievably dirty diapers, projectile spit-ups, and colicky cries—may indeed feel like a series of whirlwinds and tremors and fires. But we too may find God responding with a still small voice: a surge of love as we see our partners snuggling baby and realize that we are all truly trying our best, a sense that being pooped on is actually inexplicably yet undeniably not such a big deal after all, a renewed conviction that we can and will meet the demands of parenting our children. We may come to feel that God is watching us and supporting us—even that God is proud of us.

In the beginning there was emptiness. Only the act of Creation could fill that emptiness. But the act of Creation was not without complication, nor without challenge. Raging waters had to be gathered and tamed; light had to dispel darkness; trees had to bring forth fruit. Our act of creation is not without complication, nor without challenge. Relationships must be renegotiated and renewed; feelings and frustrations and fears must be shared (as kindly as possible) and heeded (as fully as possible); a loving space must be made not only for baby but also for each member of baby's family.

As God created the world, we are creating families. And as God beheld the Divine Creation, God proclaimed it *tov me'od*, "very good."[5] As we look at the families we—with God—have so messily, crazily, gloriously, miraculously created, may these words spring to our lips as well.

---

[4]1 Kings 19:12; the full story is related in 1 Kings 19:1–18.
[5]Genesis 1:31.

Taking Care of Your Baby

It crosses every parent's mind at some point: How can someone so small require so *much*? So much time, so much attention, so much equipment. It's incredible!

And it is undeniably true. These little creatures are completely and utterly dependent upon us, not only for love and affection but also for every basic element of human existence. Traditional morning blessings—movingly known as *Nisim Kol Yom*, "Everyday Miracles"—praise God for tending tirelessly to our needs, from granting us sight to infusing us with strength. For our children, we are God's emissaries, satisfying their needs for nourishment, for clothing, for shelter, for cleanliness, for safety.

I had never changed a diaper before my first son was born. Those early days were a disaster for me, and a blur of hilarity for my husband (a hands-on uncle of eight at that point, who knew his way around the changing table) as I managed to yank the old diaper off at the exact moment—well, you can picture the rest. I really didn't get the hang of it until my son was about five days old—which is a lot of diapers! My husband (who in the interest of fairness I must admit stepped in to rescue me at least a few times) and two nurses tutored me with varying degrees of patience, and finally it began to feel like second nature, something I'd been doing my whole life.

Eventually, caring for baby will come to feel like second nature (although every time you find yourself settling into a comparatively easy, almost-effortless rhythm, she may decide it's time for a growth spurt!) and you will find many resources to help you along the way. Inspired by Jewish teaching and my own Jewish parenting, I'd just like to add a few of my experiences, observations—and perhaps most important, encouragement.

First, please know that there will be a lot of tears in the early weeks—some from the adults (tears of frustration, tears of exhaustion, but also plenty of tears of joy) and even more from your little one. The power of these tears—and the power of the emotions they convey—may prove surprising and overwhelming; it is perhaps only a new parent who will appreciate the Jewish legend that tears are mighty enough to cool the very fires of hell.[6] And yet these cries are baby's only method of communication; he can't yet talk, obviously, and even his sweet little coos and gurgles may still be weeks away.

Over time you will become an expert at distinguishing baby's hunger cry from her dirty-diaper cry, her pain cry from her overtired cry, her emergency-I-need-help-right-now cry from her I-don't-want-that-blue-block-I-want-the-red-one cry. For now, however, each cry can sound absolutely soul-searing, provoking a rush of alarm (along with adrenaline!) as you race to tend to baby right away. Although she may be experiencing deep and genuine pain, it's far more likely that she has a wet or dirty diaper, needs to burp, wants to eat *again,* or is just trying to tell you she'd prefer to be held a bit differently (that's better but not quite right, maybe move that arm a little bit please, hey, that's not what I meant—*waaah*!).

You will hear many stories about babies who cried hysterically unless they were being driven in the car, resting in a bouncy seat on the dryer, or listening to the vacuum cleaner. They are all true; and after a few days with your own baby, any disbelief you may have had will dissipate completely. Nevertheless, before schlepping baby (and your probably exhausted self) out to the car, try a variety of more traditional methods of soothing. Some parents swear by swaddles or slings or rocking chairs; others hold baby like a football, or offer backrubs and leg massages, or stand and sway for longer than they thought possible. You might also try singing or speaking softly to baby. Whisper that you know he feels sad and that you want to help him feel better, that he is safe with you, that you will do your best to take care of him and that you love him very much.

And here comes some advice that might appear impossible to follow: Try to stay calm and in control of your emotions. Now I realize holding an inconsolable baby is hardly a recipe for serenity, and who can be blamed

---

[6]In Exodus *Rabbah* 7:4 and *Midrash Tehillim* 84:3, in Bialik 574:322.

for feeling increasingly frantic when she just will not stop screaming; but know that just by holding her and trying to respond to her cries, you are actually already doing a great job. Even if you cannot find the magic hold that stops the crying once and for all, your efforts are wonderful for your little one. You are demonstrating that you hear her and want to help her; that you value and respond to her efforts at communication; that she will not lose your love and attention by crying; and that she can count on you to hold and nurture her when she expresses sadness or pain. If you can focus on the good work you are doing, and feel justifiably proud of yourself, you will find baby's cries easier to cope with, and your own tough situation of caring for a weeping newborn easier to bear. During my middle son's four-hour afternoon crying jags (I am not exaggerating, although I wish I were!) I used to comfort myself by reciting quietly the words of the Psalmist: "Weeping lingers for the night, but joy comes in the morning," and "You have turned my weeping into dancing...O Eternal my God, I will give thanks to You forever."[7]

A caveat: Some babies simply will not stop crying until they completely tucker themselves out. This may just be part of their personality (a part they will most likely outgrow, so don't panic about that on top of everything else!), or it may be a sign that something is not quite right. Many new parents are hesitant to "bother" their pediatrician or come off as overanxious or neurotic; but really, if you are concerned about your baby's crying, call the doctor. You will not be the first nor the last worried parent to bring in a perfectly healthy baby for evaluation; but if the crying signals an allergy, reflux, or other medical issue, you will be ensuring that your little one gets the care he needs.

Another thought: Judaism reminds us frequently of the power of community. On Yom Kippur we confess our sins not as individuals but as a congregation; one folk story compares a Jew trying to go it alone to a lonely piece of coal, unable to sustain light and warmth. And certainly we

---

[7]Psalm 30:6, 12–13, excerpted.

find this value brought to life when a new baby arrives; while her birth is a sacred milestone for her immediate family, its significance often echoes far beyond baby's home—calling forth the community's attentions and congratulations.

This phenomenon is gratifying and wonderful. That babies can bring meaning and joy to so many speaks to the magnificence of being new parents, of safeguarding new lives. The opportunity to share the wonder and happiness that our children have already brought to us is empowering and thrilling. And yet, living out these exalted ideals can pose a tremendous challenge. How to share our little ones with the communities who long to welcome them—while maintaining reasonable boundaries as a family, and reasonable expectations of ourselves?

Though we may feel blessed by family and friends ready to embrace our children, we may also feel intimidated, exhausted, or overwhelmed. This does not mean we are selfish, ungrateful, or uptight; it means simply that we are navigating our new lives as parents, and need space to do so. If you wish to limit visitors in these early weeks, that is certainly your right. Some parents set particular hours in which to welcome guests; when someone calls asking to meet baby, they simply reply, "Great, we're inviting people to come see him tomorrow between three and five in the afternoon." Most people will be understanding of such limits; a few will get upset at not being able to stop in whenever it is most convenient for them; but really, that is not your problem.

When you do have visitors, don't freak out about the state of the house, your clothes, and the like; any friend worth his or her salt will be much too busy congratulating you and cooing at baby to notice that you are covered with spit-up and that your home looks as if it has been decorated in dirty-dishes-and-early-burp-cloth style. Invite them to help themselves to drinks or snacks while you sit on the couch; everyone who visits either has been, will be, or knows someone in your shoes, and they should not expect you to serve as the perfect host. (If they do seem to expect this, don't take it personally; it's their problem, not yours. Really.)

Virtually all of your visitors are going to want to hold your little one. You need not apologize, however, for putting a few restrictions on this privilege. Anyone who's sniffling, coughing, or complaining of a tummy ache should not hold baby; this may seem obvious, but you will be surprised at how many clearly unwell people will clamor to snuggle with your child. Do not act embarrassed or offer a long-winded explanation about immature immune systems; simply smile and say, "We'd love for you to hold her when you're feeling better." (Holding your ground may be difficult, but it will be good practice for when your little one becomes a toddler!) Similarly, anyone who comes into your home smelling of cigarettes should not be allowed near your child (ideally, they should not even enter your home, though this may prove impossible). Those visitors who do meet your criteria should still remove their shoes and clean their hands; we kept a few bottles of hand sanitizer nearby so we wouldn't have to send guests into our bathroom (it was more convenient for them, plus the bathroom was a complete and utter disaster).

Once your visitors have been screened and sanitized, however, be generous with baby. Unless they are holding your little one in an unsafe way, or baby is screaming to come back in your arms, let them have their time without your hovering over them watching every move. If you are really feeling industrious, you can take a few pictures; people will be so happy to be photographed with your child, and the photos will be great for scrapbooks and albums.

Taking care of your baby may keep you busier than you ever imagined. The cycle of diapering, soothing, feeding, burping, dressing, and of course holding, rocking, loving, and cherishing—on two consecutive hours of sleep—can feel endless, and overwhelming. There is so much to be done, in fact, that there may not be enough time for thinking, time for reflecting, time for adding up each individual task into a whole that is so much greater than the sum of its parts. In the very likely case that you are far too busy doing, then, let me tell you: You are engaged in holy and sacred work.

One of Judaism's most evocative names for God is *Av*, literally Father but more inclusively translated as Parent. Before the open ark on Yom

Kippur, our holiest day of the year, we address God as *Avinu*—our Parent. When we take the Torah from the ark, we sing *"Av HaRachamim"*—Merciful Parent. In the traditional morning prayer that praises God for loving us so deeply, we call God *Avinu, Av HaRachaman*—Parent, Merciful Parent.

Nor do we simply call God our Parent and leave it at that. On Yom Kippur we implore God—our Parent—to listen to us, to keep us strong, to keep us safe. When we open the ark we proclaim our trust in God—our Parent. In our morning blessing we ask God—our Parent—to teach us and to help us learn. These are not what we might consider grandiose miracles; we are not demanding that God split the Red Sea again, for example, or appear to us once more as a pillar of cloud by day and a pillar of fire by night. What we are seeking is God's daily love and care, the affections and attentions that sustain us and make our lives significant. And when we change and clean, hold and caress, feed and soothe and safeguard our little ones, we are giving them the daily care they seek. As God does for us, we do for them.

It is deeply comforting to understand God as our Parent—One Who loves us, cares for us, nurtures and sustains us—just as we deeply comfort our own little ones by loving, caring for, nurturing and sustaining them. When we parent our children, we are doing God's work.

Taking Care of Yourself

Although it may not seem as if you have enough hours in the day even to take care of your baby, you also have another very important person to care for: yourself. Of course you want to give your precious little one your best, and of course that means sacrificing plenty of your own wants and needs. However, there must be someone looking out for you as well. Becoming a new parent entails a host of new responsibilities, new delights, and new challenges; these tremendous changes are turning your world upside-down just when you may be at, shall we say, less than peak form physically and emotionally. While stress, mood swings, and tears are absolutely to be expected, you deserve for them to be taken seriously, and you deserve support in helping to ease them.

Hopefully you are spending at least part of every day awed by the wonders of being a new parent, feeling absolutely lovestruck as you watch your child, cherishing that sweet weight snuggled against your chest, seeing the whole world reflected in those beautiful eyes. Hopefully there are many times you feel all is right in the world, that you are doing a wonderful job, that your heart is full and your life complete.

Not all moments, however, will be like these. And how could they be? Caring for your infant is a wholly new experience; even the most seasoned babysitter or hands-on aunt or uncle is still a new parent, with so much to learn and so many adjustments to make. This learning and these adjustments come when you may be feeling your most exhausted, disoriented, and vulnerable. Hormones may be raging through your body, you may be beyond sleep deprived, you may be dealing with body-image issues or family-related stress. You may feel disconnected from friends who don't have children; you may feel marginalized by friends with older children who tell you that if you think it's hard now, *just wait!* You may be worried about finances as the bills flow in and as baby continues to go through the diapers; you and your partner may feel at odds.

There are obviously plenty of reasons to account for feeling overwhelmed, anxious, sad, and just plain crazy. There are, however, some ways to help reduce the stress—and to care for yourself—even as you care for your little one.

In the Book of Exodus, Moses serves as the undisputed leader of the wandering Israelites. He is in charge of organizing a group of 600,000 (and that was just the men!) freed slaves to pass through the wilderness and prepare to conquer the Holy Land. Among his myriad duties was settling the inevitable disagreements that would arise among the people; the Torah records that he worked "from morning until evening...[deciding] between people and their neighbors, and making known the laws and teachings of God."[8] When Moses' father-in-law, Yitro, comes to visit, he expresses shock

---

[8]Exodus 18:13, 16, excerpted.

at how much Moses has taken upon himself. "The thing you are doing is not right!" he chastises. "You will surely wear yourself out, and these people as well. For the task is too heavy for you; you cannot do it alone."[9]

We cannot do it alone. We must learn to step back, to admit we need assistance, to ask for and accept help. If we try to go it alone, we will "wear [ourselves] out, and these people as well." If we try to go it alone, we will compromise ourselves and those we care for.

It can be very difficult to ask for and accept help. We may feel we should be entirely self-sufficient, that we should be able to handle this, that we are letting ourselves or those around us down by saying, "I can't do it all." We may be hesitant to entrust childcare or household tasks to people who may do things a bit differently from the way we would like. And we may worry about asking too much of others, or making ourselves vulnerable by saying to friends and family, "I need you." But for our sake—and our children's sake—we must do these things. We must ask for and accept help.

Of course, you can also find ways to help yourself. One of the most oft-repeated pieces of advice to new parents—"Sleep when the baby sleeps"—is actually one of the most helpful. You may feel silly climbing into bed at 10:20 a.m. for a little snooze; but when baby wakes up an hour or so later clamoring for your full attention, you will feel glad you did. A catnap will recharge you much more than cleaning the kitchen or going through the mail. Eating right may be too much to hope for in the first days, when you may have a hard time finding a minute even to pour a bowl of cereal, but the sooner you are able to return to at least some semblance of a healthful diet, the better your body and mind will function. Continue to follow—and to seek out—the counsel given by your obstetrician or midwife for successful postpartum healing, and be certain to schedule your three- or six-week postpartum visit.

Most of all, though, we can help ourselves by treating ourselves with the support and understanding we hope to receive from others. We wouldn't let our friends say to us, "Yeah, great, you have a new baby, but

---

[9]Exodus 18:17.

you're way behind on bills and thank-you notes. And what's that weird smell in the kitchen?" So we shouldn't say that to ourselves. This is a time to give ourselves a break from our highest expectations, a time not to concentrate on what's temporarily fallen by the wayside but to celebrate what we are—amazingly enough—able to accomplish.

However, in all of this discussion about taking care of baby and taking care of ourselves, there is still one other important person who deserves (more than) a mention. If you are blessed to have a life partner with whom to share your parenting journey, please remember also to take care of her or him.

The first year of parenthood can typically be one of the most stressful times a couple will experience, and we sometimes take this stress out on each other. For sure, some of our complaints are justified; but for sure, some of them are not. If you truly, in your heart of hearts, believe that your spouse loves you, loves baby, and is trying to do a good job by both of you, try to remember that when he or she has once again diapered baby all wrong or once again greeted you at the door sobbing that there is nothing to eat for dinner or once again managed to sleep right through baby's middle-of-the-night crying for a bottle. That is not to say that these issues are not important, or not worth discussing, or not worth even arguing about on occasion. But please recognize that as important and as immense as they seem at the moment, they are—believe it or not—only temporary. Hurtful words and unkind acts will sting much longer than the situation that gave rise to them.

Briefly and beautifully the Talmud reminds us: "Your partner is like your own person."[10] During this difficult and at times overwhelming transition, you may feel at odds, disjointed, unconnected with your spouse. And yet you are the same people you have always been, and your union is the same partnership you have so long cherished. After a few months, baby will no longer be a newborn. However, you two will still be together. Please, then, try to treat your partner with gentleness and love— to treat your partner "like your own person."

---

[10]*Menachot* 93b, in Bialik 627:154.

As our first days of being a parent turn into a week, then into weeks, ideally we grow in physical and emotional strength. While parenting will still be a challenge (even when our kids are grown and have children of their own, it will probably still be a challenge!), we should begin to feel more confident in our abilities and more natural in our new role. For some women who have given birth, however, this does not happen.

While about 50 to 80 percent (estimates vary) of all new mothers suffer the "baby blues"—a few days of mild depression or malaise that usually resolve without therapeutic intervention—others will fall prey to even more serious mental and emotional afflictions. If during the first six weeks of baby's life (even later for breastfeeding mothers), you are overcome by paralyzing anxiety, extreme difficulty sleeping and eating, or vivid images of harm coming to you or your little one, you may be among the estimated 10 to 15 percent of new mothers who suffers postpartum depression (PPD). While for many years women hesitated to seek help for PPD, fearing they would be seen as bad or "unnatural" mothers, virtually everyone now understands that PPD is a genuine and serious illness, not something you can just adjust your attitude, snap out of, or put on a happy face to avoid. Please don't be afraid to seek intervention if you recognize in yourself or in your spouse the symptoms of PPD; therapy and medication can help tremendously, and simply knowing that help is out there will lighten the load.

In *Pirkei Avot*—the Sayings of our Ancestors—are recorded the words of the ancient Sage Ben Hei Hei: "According to the labor," he taught, "is the reward."[11] This is a time of labor, and—correspondingly—a time of reward. The more care and love, the more time and energy, we give to our little ones, the more complete and whole, the more meaningful and binding, we know our family ties will be. The labor is essential, it is holy, and the reward is great.

---

[11]*Pirkei Avot* 5:26.

But we must also take a respite from our labor; and this lesson comes from no less an authority than our God. For six days, as we know, God labored in the work of divine creation, but on the seventh day God paused for rest and refreshment.[12] For minutes and hours, for days and weeks, we will labor as parents; yet we too must find time to pause, to rest, to refresh. It's what God thinks is best—and it's pretty great for us, too.

Blessed is the Creator: Prayers for Your New Family

God is always near in times of joy and times of challenge; but sometimes we need support in reaching out to God and feeling God's presence. This collection of traditional and contemporary blessings and readings includes prayers for ourselves and our children, for help and healing, for gladness and gratitude. Just as God has created each of us and each of our families to be unique, so may these words help us and our families to create our own unique relationship with the Divine.

Shehecheyanu: A Traditional Prayer for Special Moments

בָּרוּךְ אַתָּה יְיָ, אֱלֹהֵינוּ מֶלֶךְ הָעוֹלָם, שֶׁהֶחֱיָנוּ וְקִיְּמָנוּ וְהִגִּיעָנוּ לַזְּמַן הַזֶּה.

Baruch atah Adonai, Eloheinu Melech haolam, shehecheyanu v'kiy'manu v'higianu laz'man hazeh.

You are blessed, Eternal One our God, Sovereign of the world, Who has kept us in life, sustained us, and brought us to this moment.

A Prayer for Being a Parent

בָּרוּךְ אַתָּה יְיָ, אֱלֹהֵינוּ מֶלֶךְ הָעוֹלָם, שֶׁעֲשַׂנִי אָב (אֵם) בְּיִשְׂרָאֵל.

Baruch atah Adonai, Eloheinu Melech haolam, she-asani av (eim) b'Yisrael.

You are blessed, Eternal One our God, Sovereign of the world, Who makes me a father (mother) in Israel.

---

[12]Genesis 1:1–2:4.

Birkat HaGomeil: A Traditional Prayer for Deliverance from Danger

This prayer, traditionally recited seven days after childbirth, thanks God for enabling us safely to pass through a life-threatening situation. We say it surrounded by family or friends, who respond to our prayer as shown below.

בָּרוּךְ אַתָּה יְיָ, אֱלֹהֵינוּ מֶלֶךְ הָעוֹלָם, הַגּוֹמֵל לְחַיָּבִים טוֹבוֹת,
שֶׁגְּמָלַנוּ כָּל טוֹב.

Baruch atah Adonai, Eloheinu Melech haolam, hagomeil l'chayavim tovot, sheg'malanu kol tov.

You are blessed, Eternal One our God, Sovereign of the world, Who confers favor upon us and grants us every goodness.

RESPONSE:

אָמֵן. מִי שֶׁגְּמָלְךָ כָּל טוֹב, הוּא יִגְמָלְךָ כָּל טוֹב סֶלָה.

Amen. Mi sheg'malcha kol tov, hu yigmalcha kol tov. Selah.

Amen. May the One Who shows you every goodness always confer favor upon you.

A Prayer for Adoptive Parents

From Celebrating Your New Jewish Daughter, *by Debra Nussbaum Cohen.*

> We did not plant you,
> True.
> But when the season is done,
> When the alternate prayers
> For the sun and for rain are counted,
> When the pain of weeding
> And the pride of watching are through,
> We will hold you high.
>
> A shining leaf
> Above the thousand seeds grown wild
> Not by our planting,
> But by heaven.
> Our harvest.
> Our own child.

A Prayer for Bringing a Child Home

This prayer appears in the Reform home prayerbook On the Doorposts of Your House, *edited by Chaim Stern.*[1]

מַה־טֹבוּ אֹהָלֶיךָ, יַעֲקֹב, מִשְׁכְּנֹתֶיךָ יִשְׂרָאֵל!

Mah tovu ohalecha Yaakov, mishk'notecha Yisrael!

How lovely are your tents, O Jacob, your dwelling-places, O Israel!

May our home always be a small sanctuary, O God, filled with Your presence.

May this home be your sanctuary, child, a place where loving arms will cradle you, hands uphold you, and eyes delight in you.

Let this home be filled with love.

Here let the hearts of parents and children ever be turned to one another.

Here may the bonds of trust and caring keep us together as a family.

בָּרְכֵנוּ, אָבִינוּ, כֻּלָּנוּ כְּאֶחָד בְּאוֹר פָּנֶיךָ.

Barcheinu, Avinu, kulanu k'echad b'or panecha.

As a loving Parent, bless all of us together with the light of Your presence.

Rofeh HaCholim: A Traditional Prayer for Healing

רְפָאֵנוּ, יְיָ, וְנֵרָפֵא, הוֹשִׁיעֵנוּ וְנִוָּשֵׁעָה, וְהַעֲלֵה רְפוּאָה
שְׁלֵמָה לְכָל מַכּוֹתֵינוּ. בָּרוּךְ אַתָּה, יְיָ, רוֹפֵא הַחוֹלִים.

R'fa-einu, Adonai, v'neirafei, hoshi-einu v'nivashei-ah, v'haaleih r'fuah sh'leimah l'chol makoteinu. Baruch atah, Adonai, rofei hacholim.

Heal us, Eternal One, and we shall be healed; save us, and we shall be saved; and grant us complete healing from all of our afflictions. You are blessed, Eternal One, Who heals the sick.

---

[1]Chaim Stern, ed., *On the Doorposts of Your House* (New York: Central Conference of American Rabbis, 1994), 110–1.

From Psalm 20: For Difficult Moments

> May the Eternal One answer you in time of trouble,
> The name of Jacob's God keep you safe.
> May God send you help from the sanctuary,
> And sustain you from Zion.
> May God grant you your desire.
> May the Eternal One fulfill your every wish.

From Psalm 144: For Joyous Moments

> Our sons are like saplings, well-tended in their youth,
> Our daughters are like cornerstones, giving shape to a palace.
> Our storehouses are full, supplying produce of all kinds,
> Our flocks number thousands, even myriads, in our fields.
> There is no breaching and no sortie,
> And no wailing in our streets.
> Happy the people who have it so!
> Happy the people whose God is the Eternal!

3

There Was Evening, There Was Morning
Baby Days

"There was evening, there was morning, one day...there was evening, there was morning, a second day..."[1] The language is prosaic, noncommittal; it gives no hint that what lies between those indifferent words is the greatest miracle ever known: God's creation of the world.

This may, however, be the last thing on our minds as we embark upon our first year as parents. Our evenings and mornings roll by, a blur of diapering, feeding, holding, rocking, sleeping (sometimes), and not sleeping (more often). There are days spent in bathrobes, without a shower, without a proper meal or even a sense of what meal we should be eating because we have lost all sense of time. There is confusion, frustration, bickering with those we love most, a sense that we are overwhelmingly and inescapably in over our heads.

And yet within those evenings and mornings, among the challenges and exhaustion and changes, is our own holy work. The Torah recounts God's creation of the world from *tohu va'vohu*,[2] from a chaotic void; and if there

---

[1] Genesis 1:5, 8.
[2] Genesis 1:2.

is a more apt description of a household with a new baby, I have yet to encounter it. Still, it is from and with this chaos that we create our families,
from this frenzy of activity and emotion that we adjust to our new roles as
parents and fashion a sacred place in our lives for our children.

These evenings and mornings mark our own acts of creation, and
so—as Jewish folk wisdom teaches—does God's world begin anew.

Sing to God: From "The Itsy-Bitsy Spider" and "The Wheels on the Bus" to *"Bim Bam"* and *Sh'ma*

The womb is a full-service establishment. Warm and safe, it contains and
protects, nourishes and nurtures, holds close and provides room to grow.
Perhaps the only hint to baby that there is something else out there—
another world waiting to embrace her—is a voice.

Research has shown that babies can hear even while they remain in the
womb. Newborn babies appear to recognize the voices or even music they
encountered most often in utero; the sounds have served as a conduit, a connection, linking them to those who awaited their arrival. These same voices
will often guide baby through his first weeks, when his vision is lacking and
so much around him feels scary and unfamiliar. Even when we know that
they cannot possibly understand the words we are saying to them, perhaps
this is why talking—and especially singing—to our babies feels so natural.

Jewish tradition attests to the magic of song and speech. To one of the
climaxes of our people's history—God's parting of the Red Sea and our
exodus from Egypt—Moses and Miriam responded by leading the Israelites in song.[3] So sacred was that song—which included the passage traditionally chanted as the prayer *Mi Chamochah*—that Jews still rise when its
words are read from the Torah. And God longs for our own songs as well:
"Sing forth to the Eternal," exhorts the Psalmist. "Sing God a new song;
play sweetly with shouts of joy!"[4] Words, too, possess special power; they
are nothing less than the key to creation. When God began to form our

---

[3]Exodus 15:1–18.
[4]Psalms 33:1, 3.

world, the Book of Genesis relates, the only tools God employed were words: "God said, 'Let there be light,' and there was light."[5] While we may not enjoy so complete a mastery over speech, the Hebrew language reminds us that we, too, can use words in the act of creation. The Hebrew *davar* translates not only as "word" but also as "thing"—underscoring the relationship between intangible speech and tangible result. And so might we describe our earliest interactions with our children, forging a strong and true connection through the channels of speech and song.

Although there is no shortage of secular songs to sing or everyday matters to talk about with your baby, Judaism provides some wonderful and meaningful ways to connect through singing and speech. Early on, most parents develop a bedtime routine that includes a song or two; why not embrace Judaism's traditional nighttime ritual and make the *Sh'ma* the last words you sing to your child before she falls asleep? You might add a simple Shabbat song like *"Bim Bam," "Shalom Alecheim,"* or even "Sabbath Prayer" from *Fiddler on the Roof* to the repertoire on Friday nights; soon enough your little one will come to associate the extra melody—and extra time in your arms—with the warmth of Shabbat. If your child is sick, cranky, or having a hard time settling down, Debbie Friedman's arrangement of the *"Mi Shebeirach"* will prove every bit as soothing as a secular lullaby (which is to say, it may soothe your little one a great deal or not at all, depending on the situation and her temperament; but it is a beautiful prayer). There are also some wonderful, accessible Hebrew folk songs (one consists entirely of the words *"Heveinu Shalom Alecheim"*), contemporary Jewish tunes, and prayers that your baby will come to recognize and love every bit as much as "Old MacDonald" and "Five Little Monkeys." Even if you have a difficult time carrying a tune (or if you find song lyrics escaping you in these early days with baby) you can still bring Jewish music to your child's life with *nigunim*—wordless, soothing melodies perfect for humming as you prepare your little one for sleep. Search online or at your Judaica or synagogue gift shop for Jewish children's music; you may be happily surprised at the tremendous selection.[6]

---

[5] Genesis 1:3.

[6] A great resource for Jewish children's music is URJBooksandMusic.com.

Talking with your baby is another opportunity to begin—very gently—introducing him to the world in a spiritual way. Rather than just pointing out the clear blue sky, you might add, "Didn't God make a beautiful world?" Instead of just telling him how lucky you feel to be his parent, you can say, "I'm so happy that God brought you into our family!" You can sprinkle your conversation with brief references to Jewish heroes or heroines, and provide your child's earliest introduction to Jewish living: "Oh, that little boy's name is Adam—just like the first man Adam in the Torah," "You were so brave when the doctor gave you your shots, as brave as Queen Esther," or "I'm going to pick up this piece of litter and throw it away, because Judaism tells us to take care of the earth." Will your little one understand every word you say? Of course not, no more so than he at first comprehends a pet's name or his colors or whether you are pointing to the treetops or the sky; but over time, words like "Jewish," "Torah," and "God" will become as much a part of his familiar vocabulary as "doggie," "stroller," and "night-night." And while speaking like this may feel odd at first—particularly if, like most Jews today, you are unaccustomed to thinking, let alone talking, in this manner—you are giving your child—and perhaps even yourself—the incomparable gift of getting acquainted with God.

The "Mommy Wars" and Saying "No" to Guilt

It is often one of the first questions a new parent—especially a new mother—will ask another. Although it can be phrased in various ways, usually it sounds like this: "Do you stay home with your children?" or "Do you work?" If the answer matches that of the person who asked the question, the conversation tends to unfold in a relaxed, accepting atmosphere. But if the answers do not match—one parent works outside the house, another parent stays home full time—things can get complicated. The "working" parent might feel defensive, as if she needs to prove her devotion to her children, or smug, as if her career renders her superior to someone who merely sits around the house. The "stay-at-home" parent, too, might feel defensive, as if she needs to prove her worth to society at large, or smug, as if her long hours at home render her superior to someone who employs childcare.

This tension has been examined, explored, and—I would say—exploited for far too long. Long enough for it to have earned a ridiculous name—the "mommy wars"—as if parents have nothing better to do than hunker down and defend their family against a squadron of mothers who live a bit differently. And long enough that too many families think it's appropriate to regard each other's choices not with disinterested acceptance but with judgmental criticism. If you have not heard it yet, you probably will soon: "I could never leave my baby with someone else to go to work." "I would just hate to miss a single precious moment." "I would go crazy changing diapers all day." "I couldn't stand to let my education go to waste." When we react to another mother's choice in these ways, we are—intentionally or not—disparaging someone's most personal and private decision.

In ancient times, when neither of two opposing viewpoints proved able to prevail in a dispute, our Sages would concede: "*Elu v'elu divrei Elohim hayim*," "These and these are words of the living God." Neither side was wholly correct, yet neither merited nor required further argument or justification. Both opinions were accepted as fine, right, worthy; each was acknowledged respectfully, and the matter was closed. "*Elu v'elu divrei Elohim hayim*; these and these are words of the living God." It is a message we would do well to speak today.

And yet it is hard to do so. Why? I think because as much as our words might trumpet otherwise, deep down we are unsure about the choices we ourselves have made. If we give up careers to stay home with our children, we may indeed miss the adult companionship, the earned wages, the sense of contributing to and being valued by society. If we continue to work outside the house, we may indeed be torn between home and office, between achieving at work and spending time with family, between feeling like dedicated employees and dedicated parents. It's much easier to look down on the choices someone else has made—or at times been compelled to make—than to admit our own uncertainty and confusion. It's much easier to imagine that another parent is plagued by insecurity and guilt than to confront those feelings in ourselves.

And so much of parenting revolves around guilt. The feeling can begin early on—and prove surprisingly difficult to overcome. Rearing children in a society that tends to demand and evaluate rather than nurture and assist, we focus on what we are doing wrong rather than on all we are doing right; we imagine the horrible, far-reaching effects that might arise from a single parenting misstep, rather than congratulate ourselves when we do our job well (and by "do our job well," I mean sometimes simply make it through the day). Guilt becomes a habit that grows oddly familiar, even comfortable; we grow so accustomed to hearing of it, speaking of it, and feeling it ourselves that we forget how destructive it can truly be. One of my friends has the disconcerting tendency to relate her less-than-perfect parenting moments and conclude, "I'm such a terrible mother." She is no such thing, and she recognizes on one level that she is actually a wonderful mother. But there is another level on which she is not so certain, a level on which this bright, devoted woman is ruled by self-doubt, anxiety, and just plain guilt.

One of my colleagues who works full time has expressed how guilty she sometimes feels spending long hours away from home; I have told her how guilty I sometimes feel "wasting" my rabbinic training by staying home with our children. We feel guilty if our little ones don't have a plethora of engaging toys, and we feel guilty about possibly spoiling them. We feel guilty if we let our children watch a couple of videos so we can do something for ourselves, and we feel guilty if we resent our children for taking up all of our time. We feel guilty if we don't take our babies to playgroups or enrichment classes, and we feel guilty if we're overscheduling them at such a young age. We feel guilty if we leave our children with other caregivers so we can work outside the house, and we feel guilty if we are too busy tending to our children to get anything else done. Meanwhile, our children are clothed, sheltered, fed, loved, growing, and thriving. So why do we feel so terrible?

Much has been written about the reasons for parental, particularly maternal, guilt: that we spend too much time away from our little ones; that we should apply the values of giving-it-your-all and never-resting-on-your-laurels to the tasks of parenting; that children can no longer thrive without constant supervision and guidance; that we must prepare our children early on to succeed in a competitive, demanding world; that our precious and special children deserve only the best.

Most of these statements will resonate with us. However, their combined impact is dismaying, dispiriting, demoralizing. They leave us with a sense that whatever we do is not enough. And how could it be? In order to work to support our families or to fulfill our own potential, we must spend time away from our children. We cannot give our children our all, every moment of every day, and have energy left for our deserving partners, friends, and selves. We can—and should—encourage and educate our children, but we cannot know for certain what their capacities will be, or if they will choose to fulfill them. And as much as we love and cherish our little ones, we must acknowledge that there will be times they will receive less than the best.

If we try to live up to these impossible ideals, we will meet with failure, disappointment, and—of course—terrible guilt. Judaism, however, counsels us to do otherwise. Judaism encourages us to set these unreachable goals aside and—rather than feel guilty about what we cannot do—take pride in what we can do, and do well.

First, let us differentiate between reasonable guilt and unreasonable guilt. Some of our guilt may in fact be reasonable, may guide us to recognize real shortcomings and make essential changes. Perhaps we are truly too busy outside the house and need to carve out more time for our spouses and children. Perhaps we feel overwhelmed by our babies and need help in coping. Perhaps we find ourselves covering up our insecurities about parenting by lashing out at our partners or turning away from our little ones. In such cases, guilt is a useful tool, an inspiration to examine and mend our ways. Yet even then, guilt should quickly give way to action, then be entirely discarded.

In contrast to the stereotypes conjured by Jewish mother jokes and the phrase "Jewish guilt," Judaism actually counsels against excessive guilt. As a nineteenth-century Chasidic passage, read in preparation for Yom Kippur, the Day of Atonement, reads: "What is the use of weighing and measuring our [shortcomings]? In the time I am brooding on this, I could be stringing pearls for the joy of heaven…Do not brood [but] do good. You have done wrong? Then balance it by doing right."[7] Rather than ruminating endlessly on our deficiencies, we can put them in the past and let ourselves begin anew. Rather than waste our energy "brooding"— castigating ourselves and immersing ourselves in guilt over our failures— Judaism teaches us to "string pearls for the joy of heaven"—to find a new, more right, path that will bring joy to us and those we love.

It is likely, however, that much of our guilt is unreasonable—the result of ridiculously bloated expectations of ourselves as parents and our quite predictable inability to meet them. Let me give an example: When I was pregnant with our second child, I was overjoyed—yet simultaneously, I was consumed with guilt. There were days I was too tired to do all the things I wanted to do with our first son, then barely one year old. There were times I popped in a video instead of making block towers with him so I could lie down (on my left side, of course). There were also premonitions of more guilt to come: an awareness that he would have to share me, that I would no longer be able to focus all my parenting energy on only him, that he would miss out on weeks of playgroup and trips to the park while we adjusted to life with the new baby. When at about thirty weeks my obstetrician told me that my blood pressure was starting to creep up and that I would probably need to go on partial bed rest within a few weeks, I actually felt so guilty imagining how unavailable I might soon be to my son that instead of going home and lying down, I took him to the zoo! In retrospect, it all seems crazy. But it also seems I was not alone. Many of my girlfriends shared similarly guilt-fueled experiences. We were doing absolutely the best we could—yet we still felt guilty. This is just one type of unreasonable guilt. Unreasonable guilt is not guilt we need to explore, assuage, give into. It is simply guilt to be gotten rid of.

The eighteenth-century Rabbi Zusya of Hanipoli offers this wisdom: "In the world to come, [God] will not ask me, 'Why were you not Moses?' [God] will ask me, 'Why were you not Zusya?'"[8] Moses was the pre-

---

[7]In Stern, *Gates of Repentance*, 240.
[8]In Klagsbrun, 6.

eminent of all Judaism's Sages and prophets: wise, brave, compassionate, the only person to merit seeing God and speaking with God as we speak with our friends. But God does not expect every rabbi to be like Moses. Similarly, God does not expect us to be preeminent parents: always sure of ourselves, always energetic, always all-giving. God asks only that we be our best selves, that we live up to the best within us. God does not expect perfection. And if our Creator does not expect us to be perfect, why should we expect it of ourselves?

If we have any lingering doubts, let Rabbi Zusya's contemporary, Rabbi Elimelech of Lyzhansk, dispel them. He explains: "When I die and stand in the court of justice, they will ask me if I had been as just as I should have. I will answer no. Then they will ask me if I had been as charitable as I should have been. I will answer no. Did I study as much as I should have? I will answer no. Did I pray as much as I should have? And this time, too, I will have to give the same answer. Then," he concludes, "the Supreme Judge [God] will smile and say: 'Elimelech, you spoke the truth. For this alone you have a share in the world to come.'" Now, had Rabbi Elimelech been a terrible person, admitting to cruelty, deceit, and unkindness, presumably his truthfulness would not have been enough to earn God's approval. But Rabbi Elimelech was a good man. He was wise, kind, and patient. He strove for justice and charity, devoted himself to study and prayer. Yet he was sensitive enough to realize that it is impossible to do as much as we should, to give our best 100 percent of the time. And he was insightful enough to apprehend that that's okay.

While Judaism guides us always to nurture the divine potential within us, it simultaneously reminds us that we are flesh and blood, prone by nature to missteps and mistakes. God understands that; after all, it's the way we were created. And if God is not in the business of heaping guilt upon us for our every shortcoming, surely we can give ourselves—and one another—a break as well. Once we recognize that none of us is perfect, that each of us is just trying to do the best we can, joining in the "mommy wars" may not seem so appealing. Let's use our energy instead as Judaism counsels—to be honest with and accepting of ourselves, and to grow comfortable not with the flawless parents we think we should be, but with the good-enough parents we actually are.

Thus Far Shall You Come, and No Farther: The Beginnings of Boundaries and Discipline

Most of us say it when our children are newborns: "The baby won't let me!"

Maybe you want to take a shower, but as soon as you get the water running and the baby settled in the bassinet nearby, she decides she's hungry. Maybe you've nursed her and rocked her to sleep, but if you try to slip her into the crib, her eyes fly open and she begins screaming. Maybe she's happy in her bouncy seat, but just as you take out the pots and pans to start cooking dinner, she opens her little arms and whimpers to be held. It seems true: The baby won't let me shower, won't let me put her down, won't let me get dinner ready!

Of course, it's not really the babies running the show—it's us. If we wanted to, we could ignore our crying children and get in the shower, or leave them in their cribs, or continue cooking…but we probably don't. Newborns (defined as babies up to age three months) thrive on as much immediate attention as we can provide; they are learning to trust, learning to communicate, learning that their wants and needs—and therefore their own selves—are important. So hungry one-month-olds need us more than we need a shower; eight-week-olds with outstretched arms tend to trump home-cooked dinners.

Countless experts and parents have weighed in on how long this phase should last, and when—if ever—a parent should establish a regular schedule for baby's feeding, sleeping, and playtime. For the first four to six months, I believe strongly in following baby's schedule as much as possible: feeding him on demand, picking him up when he cries, soothing him to sleep if he is unable to drift off on his own. Yes, it is exhausting—I've done it three times and still remember the fog of sleep deprivation and the 2:00 A.M. panic that this baby would never go to bed—but it does end and it does matter. While essentially putting our own needs (including regular sleep!) on hold for several months is no small sacrifice, it is also not too steep a price to pay for an attached and trusting infant.

Almost as important as centering life around baby's every want and need for the first few months, however, is remembering that this phenomenon must at some point stop. A newborn should feel that she's the focal point of the universe, but a seven-month-old should be learning that she occupies an essential but not central place in the world. While it may be fine to say about a two-month-old, "She won't let me put her down" (it means that she prefers to encounter the world or take a rest in her caregiver's arms, and that her caregiver knows to indulge her), it's not so great to be saying—and genuinely meaning—about a twelve-month-old, "She won't let me change her diaper."

How, then, do we get from point A—arranging every waking and sleeping moment around our babies—to point B—teaching that actually, they are not emperors and empresses of the galaxy after all? I think it all stems from one of the most important concepts in parenting: the setting of boundaries.

In the biblical Book of Job, God recounts the divine command given to the oceans: "Thus far shall you come, and no farther."[9] God creates the seas and sets their waters free, to surge in waves and to crash upon the shore, to swathe much of the world and sustain countless species of life…but their reign is not absolute. Lest it overrun God's creation and destroy the balance of life God has designed, God sets limits for the ocean. God is a setter of boundaries.

In their first months of life, little ones need to know "Thus far shall you come." Through words and actions, parents teach children that they are welcome, cherished, loved. These earliest weeks help build the security and confidence that will sustain them throughout their lives, as they grow to their potential and discover how far they shall come.

Yet there are limits to how far they can go; and once a child is old enough to begin comprehending these limits, we must work to instill

---

[9]Job 38:11.

them as well. "Thus far shall you come, and no farther." I believe this is a call to teach boundaries even to our babies: the boundary between parent and child, the boundary between acceptable and unacceptable, the boundary between "yes" and "no."

We can begin setting these boundaries by using the word "no" and applying appropriate consequences for hurtful behavior. When a nursing seven-month-old bites his mother's nipple (even if he's teething), he will begin to respect boundaries when he is removed from the breast and told, "No biting." A nine-month-old who repeatedly pulls his father's chest hair and smiles at daddy's grimace will begin to respect boundaries when his father says, "No, that hurts," and puts him on the floor. An eleven-month-old who angrily throws food from his high chair tray will begin to respect boundaries when his meal is taken away.

Please understand that I am not advocating setting rigid or impossible standards of behavior for infants. At this age, little ones will fuss in public places, turn up their noses at pureed spinach, pee on us, scatter dog food all over the floor, spill just about anything—it's part of being a baby, and it's fodder for great memories we'll share when they get older. ("Tell the story about the time I spit up all over you!" my younger brother would beg my mother when he and I were preschoolers.) I also know that when we look at our wonderful, precious, angelic little ones, we may feel wrong to be thinking about issues like boundaries and discipline.

It's hard to take babies off the breast for biting—they don't really understand, and teething is so painful. It's difficult to put our little ones down on the floor instead of letting them continue to yank our hair—they seem to be enjoying it, and it doesn't hurt that much. And it's sometimes nearly impossible to look into those beautiful faces and see those vulnerable eyes well up with tears when they hear us say "no." But the alternative is to teach our children that there are in fact no boundaries—that they can do as they wish with impunity, without regard for the feelings or needs of others. Sure, a ten-month-old bopping her mother's nose is pretty cute—but a sixteen-month-old hitting playmates to see what their reaction will be is not nearly as adorable. We can understand that a twelve-month-old means no malice by flinging a block at the family cat—but we cannot excuse an eighteen-month-old who deliberately hurts her pets.

By establishing boundaries early on, you set your little one on the path of respectful—and respectable—behavior. You also teach him that as much as you love and cherish him, you—not he—are in charge, and you—not he—will make the rules by which your family lives.

"Thus far shall you come, and no farther." God speaks with encouragement—expand, flourish, and thrive—but God also defines limits, sets boundaries. Without these limits, the world could not endure; within these boundaries, there is security and growth, goodness and life.

Lailah Tov: A Regular Sleep Schedule

The Talmud records disagreement among our ancient Sages on the subject of sleep. In one passage we read: "Eight things are harmful in large quantities but beneficial in small ones"—among these eight things is sleep. (Others, incidentally, include travel, sex, wealth, wine, and hot baths.[10]) But, Rav Judah counters, "The night was created for no other purpose than sleep."[11] Often our little ones appear enamored with the wisdom of this first passage (at least with regard to sleep). How can we convince them that Rav Judah has it right?

According to studies, more than half of new mothers (and no doubt quite a few fathers as well) suffer from a sleep deficit. A sleep deficit is more than feeling tired, or wishing we could take a quick snooze at our desks; it manifests itself in physiological ways: our reflexes slow down, we have trouble concentrating, we can't control our moods and temper as we'd like. Extended sleep deprivation has even been linked to heart disease, hypertension, and diabetes.

Now I'm not saying all this to scare us. Once we have children, we have to accept that we no longer retain full control over our nighttime hours, and it will be difficult if not impossible to get as much sleep as we

---

[10]*Gittin* 70a, in Bialik 595:219.
[11]*Eruvin* 65a, in Bialik 596:227.

need every night—let alone how much we might want! But we shouldn't shrug off our own sleep needs and dismiss as selfish our desire for an uninterrupted stretch of seven hours or so. Sleeping at night is important—it's important for parents, so we can safeguard our health and function appropriately, and—once they reach the age of four to six months—it's an important skill for our children as well.

By this age, some babies have taught themselves to sleep through the night; their incredibly lucky parents say, "It just happened naturally." Other babies are content in a family bed, waking only briefly and quickly nursing back to sleep, barely rousing their grateful parents. The rest of our children, however, may seem to have missed the memo. This leaves us with a really difficult choice: Do we continue to get up with our little ones at any hour of the night, feeding, consoling, and easing them back to sleep—or do we teach them to sleep through the night on their own? And if we choose the latter, how exactly will that be accomplished?

Myriads of writers, experts, and advisers have stepped forward to answer this question. Most of their counsel runs along these lines: Teach baby the difference between day and night by keeping the lights low and your voice soft and soothing when you tend to her at night. Don't nurse, bottle-feed, or rock her to sleep; instead, put her in the crib while she's still awake but drowsy. If she cries, go to her, but don't pick her up; simply calm her with loving pats and reassurances before leaving the room so she can fall asleep on her own. Follow this pattern at bedtime and when she wakes during the night—and before long, you will have taught her to soothe herself and independently fall asleep.

If this works for you and your baby, that is fantastic. I am a little envious, but (mostly) really happy for your family. If, however, your children are like mine and many of my friends', you may find that as soon as you place that drowsy baby in the crib and leave the room, he morphs into a wide-awake screamer who grows more and more hysterical as he realizes that for all of these nice pats and quiet reassurances (which he probably cannot even hear) he is not getting picked up. So then what?

When my first child was six months old and I was still getting up with him three times a night, I asked our pediatrician, our nurse, and pretty much everyone I knew this same question. It came down to this: Either let him continue to "rule the roost" (not my words, but for all their harshness they rang pretty true) or train him to sleep during the night, even if it meant those dreaded three words: "crying it out."

It was a tough decision. I absolutely did not want to let our son cry it out. The idea went against my instincts—to run to him when he cried and help him at any cost—and my own self-image of what it meant to be a good and caring parent. So I resisted. I kept getting up, changing a barely wet diaper that I knew wasn't bothering him, nursing him even when I knew he wasn't hungry, rocking and singing until he slumped contentedly in my arms. It was so hard, but the alternative seemed harder.

Until one night, which I will never forget, when he was eight months old and woke up three times within an hour and a half. The third time, I realized I was not doing him or me (or my husband, for that matter) any favors by continuing to coax him back to sleep. He would need to learn on his own.

You, too, may decide to go down this path. Most sleep training—it sounds so much nicer to say "sleep training" instead of "crying it out," even if it's often the same thing!—involves going through a soothing nighttime routine of nursing or a bottle, a bath, a story or some songs, a prayer, a kiss goodnight—then putting baby in the crib, telling her lovingly but firmly that it is time for bed, and letting her cry until she falls asleep. Ideally, this will take only a few minutes. In practice, it may take an hour or more (if it takes a long time, many parents will go in to check on baby periodically, offering those pats and reassurances that for my children only seemed to make things worse, but which paradoxically made me feel marginally better).

It sounds absolutely barbaric, doesn't it? It feels like it, too. Before you undertake sleep training, there are two people you must consult: your pediatrician—to rule out any medical reason for night waking and to be certain your little one does not physically require sustenance during the night—and yourself. If you are not certain you can stick to the plan, it's far better not to start at all. Letting baby cry for an hour, then feeling so upset and overwhelmed you pick him up and start rocking him will confuse him terribly. He will be bewildered and miserable, not to mention very, very tired. But if you do decide to sleep train, please know that it works, and that as unbelievably difficult as the process is, both you and baby will emerge unscathed.

Try to surround yourself with support during this time—a partner who will encourage you (you'll need a few pats and reassurances yourself!), friends or relatives who have been there, even your pediatrician or nurse. Also try to find an outlet for the anxiety and stress you will be suffering as baby cries it out; some of my friends used to e-mail me during the night venting their frustration and sadness. It will be hard—so hard—but all of these things will help. And again, it will work, and you and baby will be fine.

One more piece of wisdom from our tradition: "Rabbi Simeon ben Eleazar said: 'And behold, it was very good'[12] refers even to sleep...What Rabbi Simeon, in fact, meant was that because we sleep, we are able to get up and labor long."[13] Without proper sleep, we cannot "get up and labor long"—we cannot do our best for our children or for ourselves. And without proper sleep, our children, too, cannot "get up and labor long"—they cannot play and grow and learn to their fullest potential. Teaching our children to sleep may be difficult—but that does not make it any less important.

Lailah tov—good night!

And Abraham Held a Great Feast: The First Birthday Party

One of the biggest first-year moments marks, well, the end of the first year. As baby closes in on her first birthday (how did that happen already?) your thoughts will likely turn to how she's grown, how she's blossomed—and how you can celebrate.

The first birthday party can be a small gathering (just family or close friends) or a huge blowout (family, plus close friends, plus casual friends,

---

[12]Genesis 1:31, when God proclaims the divine creation "very good."
[13]Genesis *Rabbah* 9:6, in Bialik 596:225.

plus, plus, plus!) There is no right or wrong way to throw the party—just do what feels right for you and your family. Some babies love being the center of a whirl of activity; other babies will freak out at a loud, raucous event. Some parents love organizing elaborate festivities; other parents will freak out about planning them. All you really need is your little one, some people he loves, a camera—and something yummy to eat.

No matter what size or style party you enjoy, you can mark this special time Jewishly and spiritually. Either at baby's party or in a more intimate setting, thank God for bringing your family to this sacred moment by offering the *Shehecheyanu* blessing (*shehecheyanu* literally means "keeping us in life"; isn't that beautiful? The prayer is in Chapter 2 on page 33, and in Appendix C on page 153). You might also place your hands on baby's head and invoke the Priestly Benediction (it's in Appendix A on pages 131–32, and again in Appendix C on page 150), or echo the words our matriarch Sarah spoke upon the birth of her son, Isaac: "God has brought me rejoicing; everyone who hears will rejoice with me."[14] You can even compose an original prayer praising God for the gifts and miracles of this past year. Sing not only "Happy Birthday to You" but also in Hebrew "*Yom Huledet Sameach*" (those are the only three words; they mean simply "happy birthday," and they're sung to the same tune as the English version). If baby is pretty well stocked for clothes and toys, you might invite party guests to donate what they would have given baby to a local shelter or charity. Finally, make this celebration special not only for your little one but also for you; marking the first year of parenthood is pretty important, too! While you may not need your own cake or song, consider asking someone close to you to bestow upon you the Priestly Benediction, and to ask God to continue to bless and guide you in your parenting.

The Torah relates that Abraham was the first to throw a party on the occasion of a child's milestone—he planned a great feast when his and Sarah's son, Isaac, was weaned.[15] According to legend, some guests

---

[14]Genesis 21:6. Although Sarah literally says that God has brought her *laughter* and that others will *laugh* with her, our ancient Rabbis interpreted her words as a reference to rejoicing and happiness.

[15]Genesis 21:8.

he invited ridiculed the idea that Sarah had really been able to bear and breastfeed Isaac (remember that Sarah was ninety years old when Isaac was born). To prove them wrong, Abraham "invited all the notables of that generation, even as our mother Sarah invited their wives. Each woman brought her child with her, but not the wetnurse. A miracle was then wrought for our mother Sarah—her nipples poured out milk like two jets of water, so that she was able to suckle all these children." [16]

While this may not describe your ideal birthday bash, it does demonstrate that Jews know how to throw a memorable party. May there be many more celebrations ahead—for baby and for you, baby's wonderful family.

---

[16]*Bava Metzia* 87a, in Bialik 38:37.

4

A Time to Embrace
Caring for Yourself and Your Family

The Book of Ecclesiastes (along with the Byrds) teaches: "To everything there is a season, and a time for every purpose under heav-
en...a time for weeping and a time for laughing, a time for wailing and a
time for dancing, a time for casting stones and a time for gathering stones
together, a time to embrace and a time to shun embraces."[1] The toddler
years are made for embracing: for embracing our children, of course, but
also for embracing our partners, our loved ones and friends, and re-em-
bracing God and God's creation as we rediscover the world through our
little ones' eyes.

This is a heady time, and a joyous time. Certainly there are plenty of
challenges (quite a few parents claim that the so-called "terrible twos"
begin the day after a little one's first birthday) but there are many more
amazing moments that will—corny as it may sound—warm your heart
for the rest of your life. This is a time of wonder and discovery, of mud
pies and wading pools and finger paints, of looking at bugs and asking

---

[1]Ecclesiastes 3:1, 4–5.

"why?" and dressing up, of sticky ice cream kisses and our little ones suddenly hurling themselves into our arms at a million miles an hour. This is a time to embrace—to embrace the beauty and the chaos, the excitement and the exasperation, and most of all the love that family life with a toddler is all about.

And a Time to Shun Embraces: The Importance of Time Without Little Ones

When we are knee-deep (or neck-deep, as it often seems) in life with toddlers, it can be hard to think of anything else. Their needs, their activities, their wants—and especially their moods—consume most of our waking (and some of our sleeping) hours. Ruefully we may recall life before our little ones, finding it genuinely difficult to remember how we filled all those days before they came along; and sometimes we may catch ourselves wondering a bit wistfully if we will ever have our own lives back again.

This is indeed a time to embrace life with our children—but as Ecclesiastes teaches, we also need time to "shun embraces." Of course we love our little ones, and of course caring for and being with them are our highest priorities. We want to do all we can to be the best parents we can be. But being the best parents requires—ironically enough—that we retain selves and identities apart from parenting.

It's so easy to neglect our own needs when we have toddlers. They have such a hard time sitting in restaurants, so we don't meet friends for lunch. Nearly every room in the house is littered with their toys, so we don't invite people over. We're away at work or busy managing the house so many hours that when we have free time, we want to devote every minute to our children, so we don't go to the gym or pursue our other interests. It's impossible to find a babysitter we can really trust or afford, so we don't keep up with our own medical and dental appointments, let alone enjoy an evening out with our spouses. All of this reasoning is understandable—up to a point. But when we come up for air one day and realize we have put off our friends, our hobbies, our partners, even our health all in the name of being attentive parents, we need to heed the wisdom of Ecclesiastes.

There is "a time to shun embraces." There is a time to acknowledge without embarrassment and without apology that we need time for ourselves: time to exercise; time to read; time to nourish our friendships and relationships; time simply to do what we find fun, interesting, and meaningful. It's hard to find this time—our lives are demanding and there seem not to be enough hours in the day—and perhaps even harder not to feel guilty about claiming it for ourselves. But for our children's sake, our families' sake, and—yes—even our own sake, we need time apart.

Chapter 32 of the Book of Genesis finds our patriarch Jacob serving as the ultimate caretaker of his family. Leading them away from his dishonest father-in-law Laban and back toward the Promised Land, Jacob takes full responsibility for sustaining and protecting his loved ones. When he hears that his brother Esau—who years before had vowed to kill Jacob—is on his way to meet Jacob's family, Jacob risks not only his wealth but his physical safety to shield his beloved children.

But even as Jacob demonstrated his capacity for love and courage by caring for his family, it was in an hour of solitude that he achieved his true potential. After sending his loved ones across the river Jabbok, "Jacob was left alone. And a man wrestled with him until the break of dawn, [saying], 'You have striven with God and human beings, and have prevailed.'"[2] Some of our rabbis interpret this mysterious encounter as a metaphor; Jacob, they explain, was struggling with himself, with his good impulses and his base impulses—and finally becoming the person of integrity God had intended him to be.

This experience was an essential one for Jacob, and it came when he was away from his family. For one night he was alone—alone to think, alone to reflect, alone to grapple and to act. And when he did return to his family, he returned a better, fuller, and more complete person. Jacob's time alone was good for Jacob. And it was good for those he loved.

---

[2]Genesis 32:25, 29.

When we complement our time for embracing with the occasional time to shun embraces—the occasional time to be alone—we become better, fuller, more complete people. We feel happier with our lives and more satisfied with ourselves. We speak more kindly to our loved ones, and we respond more patiently to our children. We don't resent the demands placed on us; and we don't resent our little ones for taking up all of our time, or our spouses if they manage to find some free hours of their own.

Strangely enough, we also serve our children best by demonstrating that we have interests apart from them. While we want our little ones to know how loved and important they are, it's simply not healthy for a toddler to feel that she's the only thing that matters to her parents. That's a lot of pressure for a child, and she will, in strange and subtle ways, feel the weight of the unreasonable expectation that she alone bring fulfillment to her parents' lives. As difficult as our little ones might find being left at home while we take time for ourselves, it is far worse in the long term for them to feel that all of our love, all of our time, all of our pursuits and goals center on them.

So how do we follow Jacob's example? After all, he didn't have to worry about schedules and babysitters; while his journey to the Promised Land was a difficult one, he could travel at his own pace—plus he had on hand two spouses, two concubines, and a staff of servants! But if we are willing to be flexible and creative, we too can find time for ourselves. If you are lucky enough to have family nearby or to be able to splurge on a sitter, set a date, make a plan, and stick to it. You might also talk with friends in a similar boat and consider setting up a babysitting cooperative of sorts; on a rotating basis, each parent takes an afternoon or evening for him- or herself while the rest of the parents watch the kids. Finally, enlist your spouse; if you are feeling the need for some space, he or she can certainly be expected to care for your toddler while you go out alone.

Even if you don't feel up to leaving your little one, you can still carve out some time for yourself. Try putting him to bed a little early and enjoying a date at home with your partner. Curl up on the couch and watch a movie, or eat a late dinner by candlelight—even mac and cheese left over from your little one's meal will do, as long as it's served on pretty plates. After your child's bedtime is also a great time to invite friends over for some wine, dessert, or just conversation; you're available in case your child needs you, you don't need a sitter, and it will feel so great to enjoy some adult time in your own home. This is an especially good way to reconnect with unmarried or childless friends, for whom 8:30 p.m. will seem like a reasonable time to get together and not the staggering-to-bed end of a fifteen-hour day!

One of Judaism's greatest Sages, Rabbi Hillel, famously posed a series of questions.[3] The first two: "If I am not for myself, who will be for me? If I am only for myself, what am I?" As parents, we know well that we cannot be only for ourselves. We have children, families, to love and care for, to nurture and protect. But we also know that there are times we must be for ourselves. As wonderful and precious as our children are, they cannot be the only source of meaning in our lives. We need time apart. We need lives of our own.

Of course our schedules are crazy, of course our little ones call for us, of course it's hard to make time alone a possibility, let alone a priority. But if we truly believe in the importance of me-time, if we can pursue it without guilt and without apology, it will happen. And as Rabbi Hillel's final question goes: "If not now, when?"

Whither Thou Goest, I Will Go: Coping With Separation Awareness

We may be convinced of the importance of time for ourselves. Our children, however, may feel quite differently.

Separation awareness (the term sounds better than separation anxiety, but it means the same thing) is a perfectly normal part of our children's development—but that may be cold comfort when they break into torrents of sobs and clutch desperately at our ankles as we prepare to leave the house. Beginning in late infancy, peaking during the second year, and

---

[3]*Pirkei Avot* 1:14.

usually resolving by age three, separation awareness is an enduring challenge for both parents and little ones.

What causes separation awareness? How can our sociable children go from giggling and holding their arms out to complete strangers to burying their faces in our necks and weeping when our friends smile at them? The onset of separation awareness actually signals an important developmental milestone: Children realize that they are not merely extensions of their parents, but separate and unique individuals. What we might think would be an exciting and liberating discovery, however, can frighten our children deeply. Attached to us they feel safe; if they are not attached to us, are they still safe? What if we leave them behind and never return?

It seems so obvious to us: We might go away for a little while, but we will always return to our little ones. And when we are apart from our children, they are unquestionably safe—we would never leave them for even a moment if we thought otherwise. But while we understand this with every fiber of our being, infants and young toddlers do not; they are simply incapable of comprehending these complex truths at such a tender age. Only with patience and appropriate action—as well as plenty of time—will our little ones overcome their separation anxiety, and emerge as confident and complete individuals. That's what this phase is all about.

How can we guide them through this important but trying time? First of all, by understanding that their anxiety is not "bad" or "bratty" behavior, or something they can be talked or, worse, shamed out of, or the result of something we've done wrong. It is their way of trying to cope with the task of becoming separate people, of developing lives of their own. And we can help them along the way. First, we can engage in activities that teach what's called "object permanence"—that just because something disappears from view doesn't mean it's gone forever. Playing peekaboo; hiding a toy under a blanket, then challenging our children to find it; even leaving the room briefly but calling or singing to them so they know we are still nearby all assure our little ones that things—and people—can go away and come back. But equally essential is encouraging our children to feel confident apart from us. One easy way to begin instilling this value: Rather than telling our little ones, "I'm so proud of you! You're my special girl!" or "You're making me so happy!" we can encourage them to own and celebrate their achievements: "You did it! You must be so proud," or "You're really working hard to solve that puzzle!" Although the change in wording is subtle, it conveys an attitude that we see our children as separate individuals, and that that is a good thing.

Many children also turn to "loveys," or security objects, during this time. These can be enormously helpful. Stuffed animals, dolls, blankets, and pacifiers can all help little ones soothe themselves and feel safe in difficult situations. To children, these security objects come to represent their parents, serving as reminders of our presence and symbols of our love even when we are physically apart. Although some parents feel embarrassed or exasperated when their two-year-old still wants a pacifier, or carries his tattered blanket to daycare every morning, it's really not about us—it's about respecting our children's development and needs during this time.

And—as counterintuitive as it might sound—we can help our children most by doing what they seem to fear most: leaving them behind. Be certain you and your little one both know and trust her caregiver, and give your child a bit of notice that soon you will be leaving: "I'm going to finish reading you this story, and then I need to go out for a little while. Miss Irma will take care of you while I'm gone. She'll play with you and give you lunch and help you take your nap. After your nap I will come back, because I always come back." If your child erupts in hysterical tears, stay calm and reassure her in a matter-of-fact voice: "I hear you're upset and scared that I'm leaving. But you are safe with Miss Irma. I promise you will be safe, and I promise I will come back." (When leaving a child with a caregiver is a routine occurrence, many families create rituals to ease the transition and remind little ones that we "will always come back.") When it is time to walk out the door, walk out no matter how much your little one is carrying on. It may be difficult—heartbreakingly so—to do, but canceling your plans because "she's just so upset" or rushing back for "one last hug" are actually much worse. Those actions signal to your little one that maybe there really is something to fear, that maybe you believe she isn't safe without you either.

In the biblical Book of Ruth, we meet Ruth and Naomi. Escaping famine in the Jewish land of Judah, Naomi brought her husband and two sons to Moab. There she was widowed, and there her children married Moabite women named Orpah and Ruth. After Orpah and Ruth's own husbands died, Naomi prepared to bid farewell to her daughters-in-law and return to Judah. But Ruth refused to remain in Moab without Naomi.

"Do not urge me to leave you, to turn back and not follow you," Ruth begged. "For wherever you go, I will go; wherever you lodge, I will lodge; your people shall be my people, and your God my God."[4]

Judaism praises Ruth's loyalty, which merited her becoming the ancestress of the exalted King David and—according to tradition—the Messiah. But just as remarkable as Ruth's loyalty is her courage. Her "whither thou goest, I will go" is not the desperate call of a fearful child, but the bold act of a confident woman. Ruth understands what she must do, and she is willing to separate from virtually everything she knows—her homeland, her faith, her family of origin—in order to fulfill her destiny.

The story of Ruth actually illuminates not our children's desire to cling to us, but our children's need to flourish apart from us. Without successful separation, there can be no growth. Clinging to us, our children cannot become the people they are meant to be.

And as incredible as it may seem, the seeds of Ruth's self-assurance are sown in these early years. Responding properly to our children's separation awareness, we teach them that they can be safe and secure without us, that they can have their own experiences, their own feelings, their own wants—their own lives. And we teach them to say not to us but to whatever person or purpose comes to give their life meaning: "Whither thou goest, I will go."

People of the Book: Reading, Observing, Imagining, and Learning

Did you know that the phrase "People of the Book" originates in the Koran? Although the term applies to members of any pre-Islamic mono-

---

[4]Ruth 1:16. The previous paragraph summarizes Ruth 1:1–16.

theistic religion, it has come to be particularly associated with Jews. It certainly reflects Jewish self-perception; education has stood among our highest values for generations. On a practical level, literacy and learning enabled our forbearers to achieve success in new lands—and sometimes even a measure of success in hostile ones. On a spiritual level, however, study is just as essential. Even our prayer book prescribes a daily recitation of ethical commandments—from honoring parents to welcoming guests to visiting the sick—that concludes, "But the study of Torah is equal to them all."

Our little ones may be a long way from studying the Torah and acquiring the knowledge of their ancestors. But they are at just the right stage to become what we might call "Children of the Book"—lovers of books and all that goes with them: reading, observing, imagining, and learning.

We know how important it is to read to our children—and how much fun! Snuggling up with a book may be one of the most delicious privileges of parenthood; the fact that we are simultaneously igniting our children's imaginations, sharpening their intellect, and laying the groundwork for literacy is just a bonus. As our children grow, they can engage more and more in the reading experience, from pointing out specific illustrations to explaining what they would have done in the character's situation. Encouraging our children's participation and involvement guides them to become active learners, to see themselves as questioners and thinkers worthy of being heard. We can model reading for them as well; when our little ones see us captivated by a book of our own, we reinforce the message that reading is worthwhile—and fun.

We can also model and reinforce certain values with the books we choose. Our children are so impressionable, so malleable, and what we may see as simply the words to a classic story will affect them deeply. Make an effort to find books that reflect your ideals, and don't be afraid to change a few words here or there as necessary. One of my best friends humored her princess-loving daughter by reading *Cinderella*, *The Little Mermaid*, and all the rest—but altered the endings so that the princess and her prince became good friends and went to college together before getting married. It had a definite effect; her little girl still aspires to be "a princess radiologist"!

Reading books is, of course, a wonderful way to explore Judaism with your children. Appendices A and B contain lists of stories centering on Shabbat and the Jewish holidays. Illustrated children's Bibles and books about God, Israel, and especially Noah's ark are widely available and enjoyable anytime.[5] Add a few of these stories to your child's regular rotation of books; they will introduce your little one—and maybe even you—to the beauty and excitement of Jewish life.

As you read and share books with your child, you may notice him demonstrating an interest in how language works. If he responds excitedly to your pointing out As, Bs, and Cs, you may want to introduce him to the wonders of the alphabet. Simple books, blocks, refrigerator magnets, and even cookie cutters can be fun tools, or you can get creative—writing out letters in finger paint or pudding, jumping to the rhythm of the ABC song, or sketching the alphabet outside in sidewalk chalk and naming letters for your child to run to. Different children possess different learning styles, and you will rapidly discover if your child responds best to visual, auditory, or kinesthetic instruction.

Let me repeat myself: *Some* children will demonstrate an interest in how language works. Some will not. If your little one grabs a toy or even runs away when you try to inform her that A is for apple, please don't worry—and please don't force her to come back, or try to cajole her into "just a few more letters." The spate of toys, flashcards, and DVDs that purport to fast-track our children's intellectual development—as well as competitive parents who love to talk up their little ones' aptitude for language—can make us feel tremendous pressure to get our kids recognizing letters or sounding out words before they reach pre-kindergarten. But really, what is the point if our children don't enjoy it? There is plenty of time for them to learn to read, and the supposed advantages of early reading may dissipate by elementary school when those "slow" readers catch up anyway. Rather than teaching our toddlers and preschoolers to read books, we should be teaching them to enjoy books. And, as our little

---

[5]Jewish Lights Publishing, Jewish Publication Society of America, Kar-Ben Publishing, and URJ Press, among others, have extensive and generally excellent offerings for young children.

ones will be happy to demonstrate, there are so many ways to enjoy a book besides actually learning to read it.

When you finish reading and talking about a book with your little one, invite him to explore it on a different level. Maybe he can draw a picture of an event from the story, or build the character's house out of blocks, or use puppets, dolls, or even trucks to act out the plot. If the story takes place in the ocean, fill a bucket with water and do some splashing; if the story involves games or sports, throw a ball around; if the story focuses on cooking, head to the kitchen. Some of my children's favorite books sparked an art project that taught them to mix colors to create a new one (*Pig and Duck Buy a Truck*, by Lee Lorenz, published by Little Simon); a surprisingly educational field trip to the produce section of the grocery store (*Eating the Alphabet*, by Lois Ehlert, published by Harcourt Big Books); a matzah scavenger hunt (*Where is the Afikomen?* by Judye Groner and Madeline Wikler, illustrated by Roz Schanzer, published by Kar-Ben Publishing), and the assembly of a volcano from baking soda and vinegar (*Amelia Bedelia, Rocket Scientist*, by Herman Parish, illustrated by Lynn Sweat, published by HarperTrophy). Even before your child knows how to read books, he will know how to learn from them.

Of course, not every reading session will—or even should—inspire such a flurry of creativity. While it's great to suggest some follow-up activities, let your child take the lead in deciding which, if any, to undertake. The most important thing is not that she explore or learn anything specific—it's that she feels able to explore and learn on her own level, at her own pace.

This is, I think, an essential notion to bear in mind during these toddler and preschool years. It's really a corollary to the lesson that we need not worry about imparting reading skills to a young child who couldn't care less. As our little ones hit the ripe old ages of two, three, and four, a huge array of enrichment activities will open up to them—from academic preschools to tutoring, from art, ballet, music, and tumbling to soccer, tae kwon do, gymnastics, and swimming. If you and your child try out a couple of these classes and genuinely enjoy them, terrific! They can be a wonderful way to meet people and a chance for your child to begin acquiring some new skills. But if they're not your family's thing, that's fine too. We often hear so many voices extolling the virtues of giving our little ones a head start and affording them every opportunity that it's easy to feel guilty if we don't sign our children up for a bunch of activities. But unless your child has special or therapeutic needs, he simply does not require any of these classes in order to reach his full potential.

In fact, too much emphasis on these sorts of activities can actually hinder our little ones' learning. One of the greatest gifts we can give our toddlers and preschoolers is unstructured time—time with no agenda and no goals, time simply to play, be outside, look at books, draw, climb, pretend, even be bored. Such time teaches our children to entertain and educate themselves, to develop and deepen their own ideas. Too many structured, adult-led classes—no matter how wonderful—deprive children of this sacred time, of the opportunity to discover and learn by themselves, about themselves.

We are proud to be the People of the Book. And we are proud that Judaism not only emphasizes learning, but that it guides us to make learning a sweet experience for our little ones. In the medieval *Sefer HaKoreah*, the German rabbi Eleazar of Worms describes how small children are taught the *alef-bet*, the Hebrew alphabet: "And the rabbi reads every letter of the *alef-bet* and the child repeats after him...And the rabbi puts a little honey on the slate and the child licks the honey from the letters with his tongue."[6] Imagine how much fun it is to learn the ABCs when you get to lick honey from the letters! The pleasure—the sweetness—of reading and learning is what we want to give our little ones. And when we provide the support, the encouragement, and the gentle guidance they need, our children will indeed read and learn—and they will come to love reading and learning.

Not by Bread Alone: Family Mealtimes

In the Book of Deuteronomy, Moses reminds the Israelites that we "do not live by bread alone, but that [we] may live by anything God decrees."[7]

---

[6]Paragraph 296, cited by Rabbi Professor David Golinkin.
[7]Deuteronomy 8:3.

Although the original context of this passage recalled God's devotion during the Israelites' wilderness wanderings, today the phrase often invokes the need for something deeper—something more meaningful—than mere sustenance of the body.

Of course, for parents of toddlers, merely sustaining the body may pose a sufficient challenge. This can be the age of picky eating, or—as it seems sometimes—of virtually no eating. This is the age of an impossibly short tolerance for sitting, and of plenty of fidgeting when they do. This is the age when we might be tempted to feed our little ones anything, anytime, anywhere, just as long as they eat.

Does this sound familiar? You secure your toddler in her high chair or booster, join her at the table, and present her with her dinner. She doesn't like the looks of it, and you grab the plate just before she can sweep it to the floor. You coax her to try just a little, to no avail. Lest she miss the meal completely, you hurry to the kitchen to cook up some plain pasta (sure, we can't live by bread alone—but most of our little ones would be thrilled to try living by plain pasta alone!) or scramble an egg. By the time you return, your own meal is cold, and she's ready to get down anyway. So you end up following her around, trying to poke a few forkfuls of dinner in her mouth as she scoots from activity to activity. If she wants to eat later, you give her some graham crackers or a banana before bed—after all, you don't want her to go to sleep hungry.

Too often, family mealtimes do not serve as respite from the day's hassles; rather, they provide another—perhaps even bigger—battleground. But it does not have to be this way—in fact, it really should not be this way. Just like us, our children cannot thrive "by bread alone." Rather than focusing our energies primarily on coaxing food into our little ones, we can begin teaching them the significance of family meals—the structures, the expectations, and—yes—the joys of eating together. A family Shabbat dinner can provide an especially wonderful opportunity to instill these values—Appendix A will guide you in creating a meaningful and age-appropriate experience for your child.

It may help first to define what our real responsibilities for meals are—and what they are not. The Talmud actually sets our charge out quite clearly: "Your own sustenance has priority over the sustenance of your household," our Sages advise.[8] Yes, it is important that our children eat, and enjoy eating—but we, the parents, are entitled to pleasant and nutritious dining as well. Our little ones' enjoyment of a meal should not come at our own expense.

How can we put this teaching into practice? I believe we do so by recognizing the boundary between our children's legitimate need for nutritious, appealing food—and their less-legitimate desire to eat food of only one color, or one texture, or one taste (usually sweet), or to eat while running around the house, or while standing on a chair, or while screeching. I believe we do so by making mealtime fun for our little ones—involving them in food preparation, being patient and encouraging as they sample new dishes, offering at least one thing they will recognize and enjoy—while remembering that we are more than caterers and eating coaches. I believe we do so by balancing concern for our children's mealtime experiences with concern for our own.

When you take this attitude, mealtimes will become infinitely less stressful. You can give your little one his food, recite *HaMotzi*,[9] and cheerfully name all the items on the plate. If he digs in, terrific. If he fusses or tries to throw his food, remove it from his reach and matter-of-factly say, "I see you're not happy with this dinner, but this is what is for dinner. In just a minute, I'll give it back to you so you can eat." Let him watch you begin enjoying your own meal, then return his plate. He will probably be more receptive this time around, but if not, don't freak out. Simply say, "You don't have to eat it, but this is the only food you will get tonight. If you're hungry, you should try it." Then let him make his choice. If he eats, great (and after a few meals like this, he will)—but if not, don't worry; just take away the plate. If you want him to remain at the table, offer a small toy (nothing too exciting; don't reward him for rejecting the food) or board book that will amuse him until the adults have finished their own meals.

---

[8]*Hullin* 84a, in Bialik 587:120.

[9]The blessing appears in Appendix C. After a meal, recite the traditional blessing found in Appendix C, or simply its conclusion, *"Baruch atah Adonai, hazan et hakol,"* "You are blessed, Eternal One, Who gives food to all."

If these steps enrage your child (I really should say "when"—a few power struggles are all but inevitable), try to remain calm and confident. You can acknowledge an outburst by telling your little one, "I see you're angry about your meal," but don't try to cajole or soothe her—and definitely don't reward the behavior by letting your little one get down and play. If the yelling continues, simply say, "It's okay to be angry, but you can't scream at the table. If you continue to scream, I'll move your chair away until you calm down." Then move your little one's seat a few feet away (you'll still be able to hear every decibel of the tantrum, but it's symbolic) and try to go on about your business. If several minutes pass and she's still howling, say loudly enough that she can hear, "Well, I'm all finished. *Baruch atah Adonai, hazan et hakol.* You are blessed, Eternal One, Who gives food to all." Then tell her, "The meal is over. I'll help you get out of your chair, and hopefully we'll have a better time tomorrow."

Is this easy? No, not at all. And it can be very, very unpleasant. In the short term, you will have a much simpler time if you serve your little one his preferred food at every meal and respond to tantrums by offering an even more delectable alternative. Unfortunately, this will drive you crazy, as well as teach your child two lessons he probably should not learn: that he is the boss at mealtimes, and that tantrums produce desirable results. In the long term, instilling mealtime values and behavior is a much better bet. And even though it might seem premature to be occupied with such things early in the toddler years, doing so will head off lots of misbehaviors—from jumping up and down in the chair to yelling, "Gross! I won't eat this!"—that otherwise tend to crop up later.

Although a single unsuccessful meal can seem to last a hundred years, it really will not take long for our little ones to understand and display reasonably acceptable behavior at meals (the-napkin-in-the-lap and no-elbows-on-the-table rules can wait). And as our children learn these behaviors, they also come to learn their place in the family, and the family's expectations and values. And really, that's what mealtime is all about—being together and enjoying one another as a family. Ideally, mealtime provides sustenance not just for the body, but also for the soul. It should be a special time.

With hectic schedules, demanding jobs, and a little one who may be in bed before you or your partner gets home from work, it's difficult to make shared meals a priority. But one family meal every day is worth fighting for. It need not be dinner; breakfast will do just as well. What's important is that everyone comes together not just for food but also for companionship and conversation. Signal the beginning of the meal with a prayer—you may wish to augment the traditional *HaMotzi* by listing things for which you are grateful, or asking God to continue caring for your family, or mentioning loved ones who are on your mind—then thank whoever prepared the food. Soon enough your toddler will be able to join in these rituals by saying *"amen"* to the blessing and "thank you" to the chef; even if all the chef did was pour cereal, thanks are still in order. Try to include your child in the conversation; even if she is too young truly to participate, she will delight in having you turn to her and say, "Don't you agree, sweetheart?" or in hearing her name mentioned as you describe the day's events or share a story about something cute she's been doing lately. If she's sitting or eating nicely, or making noises that approximate "please" when asking for more food or drink, be sure to tell her how much you appreciate her good manners; a little praise can go a long way in encouraging this conduct.

Some of ancient Judaism's most amusing stories center around meals. There are accounts of two revered rabbis chastising one another for bad table manners;[10] an innkeeper who kept tasting the wine he offered a rabbi, much to the rabbi's dismay;[11] a rabbi who scolded a guest for using a piece of bread to prop up an uneven soup bowl;[12] and a rabbi's teaching that failing to wash hands before a meal was tantamount to being "rooted out of the world."[13] Apparently, mealtimes have rarely been without controversy. But mealtimes—as we know well—are also a

---

[10]*Nedarim* 49b, in Bialik 591:157.
[11]*DER* 9, in Bialik 592:166.
[12]*DER* 9, in Bialik 592:161.
[13]*Sotah* 4b, in Bialik 594:193.

source of pleasure and of sharing, and a wonderful way to nurture both body and soul.

May you and your family be sustained not by bread alone—but also and always by one another.

Like Seeing the Face of God: Keeping Faraway Relatives Close

Not so long ago, a faraway relative meant a family member who had gone out to run an errand. Although some of us still live near members of our extended family, many parents are bringing up children far away from our own parents and siblings. Of course we want our children to know and love their grandparents, aunts, uncles, and cousins, but how can we forge and nurture these relationships? Or, if we live closer to one side of the family, how can we be certain the other side is not forgotten?

Technology, of course, has made this task infinitely easier. Cell phones render long-distance calls extremely affordable—as in, virtually free— and many children enjoy at least babbling into the phone for their appreciative and hopefully very patient audience. (I actually have my parents on my cell phone speed dial, and my children know it; many times they have helped themselves to my phone, pressed the number 3, and started chattering away without my even realizing what was going on!) Maintaining a blog or e-mailing photographs, links to videos, scanned artwork, or quick notes about what our little ones are up to also helps us check in with distant relatives; webcams can offer "virtual" visits as well. Although our own parents may not yet possess all the skills needed for keeping in touch online, there is nothing like the promise of increased contact with grandchildren to inspire them to learn.

As fantastic as these innovations are, we may still wish to embrace some of the more old-fashioned methods for keeping faraway relatives near. Although e-mail has all but eclipsed snail mail for staying in touch, receiving a postcard or letter is still such a thrill for little ones. Even if your toddler can't recognize words yet, he will understand that the piece of mail is meant for him, and he will love tearing the envelope open to get at whatever is inside. Ask grandparents, aunts, and uncles to send brief notes, photographs, drawings, or artwork made by young cousins as often as they can—and be certain to send along your child's own pictures and scribblings.

Loved ones can also send videos, audiotapes, or sound files of themselves reading your little one's favorite stories, then saying "I love you" and "goodnight," for you to play at bedtime. This is even more special if your child has a copy of the book being read, and can turn the pages and follow along as she listens. Even though her relatives won't be there physically, your child can still enjoy their presence and feel their love as the day comes to a close. This tradition can also be a wonderful way to mark time Jewishly; ask family members to read special stories to help your little one prepare for holidays or learn a little bit about Israel or the Hebrew language. (You will find lots of suggested titles in Appendix B.) And when your child gets old enough to make up her own stories, she can work with her faraway family to create their own books; staple together some sheets of paper, write down a sentence or two that she dictates, and let her illustrate the first page—then send it to your loved ones, and ask them to complete page two and send the book back. After a few weeks of this, you will have—if not a coherent story—at least a wonderful keepsake.

Most of all, we help faraway relatives find a special place in our children's lives when we make them part of our little ones' everyday world. Be sure your toddler hears about and sees (at least in photos) his grandparents, aunts, uncles, and cousins every day. You can accomplish this in so many easy, fun ways: pictures hung on the refrigerator or a placemat crafted from a laminated collage of family photographs, a family portrait as a computer screensaver, or a little photo album your child can thumb through. You can tell stories about your extended family, incorporate them into songs ("Uncle Brian in the dell...Aunt Paige in the dell...") was a favorite at our house!), and add their names to the list you recite of people who love them ("Mommy and Daddy love you so much, Grandma and Grandpa love you so much, your cousins Maha and Amir love you so much...") These ideas, of course, are just the beginning; each family's unique character and traditions will give rise to unique ways of staying in touch.

Shabbat can also serve as the perfect focus for a weekly remembrance of faraway family. You might institute a Friday phone call so relatives can wish your child "Shabbat Shalom" or offer a blessing long-distance, light an extra candle on Shabbat and holidays and explain to your little one that the other candlestick is being used at that very moment at her grandparents' house, or symbolically set aside pieces of challah for faraway loved ones. Not only will rituals like these help your little one grow more familiar with her relatives, but they will also make her grandparents, aunts, uncles, and cousins part of her Shabbat, part of her Jewish observance and identity.

Of course, not all contact with distant family members will take place across the miles. Visits are an essential part of forging and renewing the bonds of family. There is truly no substitute to physically being with our loved ones—hugging, sharing meals, going on outings, and just enjoying one another. And our little ones will get to know their extended families best by spending time with them—playing, reading, and simply being together. A good visit can be so wonderful, so uplifting; such was the emotion our patriarch Jacob expressed upon visiting—and reconciling—with his brother Esau: "Seeing your face is like seeing the face of God."[14]

Yet visits alone may not bridge the distance gap as much as we would hope. Visits can be joyous, but they can also be difficult. When we are accustomed to living apart from our parents or siblings, and we suddenly experience a few days of very intense togetherness, it's easy for squabbles to arise or for old issues to crop up anew. Often visits center on holiday celebrations, which bring their own stress and which may not allow us the relaxed, unstructured time we need to strengthen our bonds. And though their grandparents, aunts, uncles, and cousins are familiar and beloved figures to us, our little ones may see them as strangers to be approached with uncertainty or wariness.

---

[14]Genesis 33:10.

Here, too, Judaism encourages us. Our ancestors, after all, grew up in families with plenty of issues and dysfunction; our dynamics are likely nothing compared to those of Abraham—who fathered a son with his maidservant, then cast her and the child out at his wife Sarah's insistence, only to see his wife perish after he nearly offered their son as a sacrifice to God—or Jacob—who manipulated his twin brother into handing over the birthright, joined forces with his mother to trick his blind father into granting him his brother's blessing, fled in fear that the spurned brother would slaughter him, and ended up marrying two sisters and fathering sons by four different women! It's pretty significant, then, that despite such challenging (to put it mildly) origins, Jewish tradition emphasizes the centrality and the holiness of honoring our family.

We may indeed find legitimate objections to the way our parents and in-laws interact with our little ones. Some relatives are prone to spoiling, to overindulging, to caring less about our children's getting balanced meals than giving them those cookies they've been asking for (and asking for...). And others appear to hold unreasonable expectations for children, insisting on perfect table manners, all-day-long quiet voices, not touching the shiny, colorful baubles that decorate just about every available surface. While these experiences would be difficult enough on their own, they may also rekindle unpleasant memories about the way we were treated as children, or intensify already-existing tension between us and our in-laws.

How to decide when to intervene, and when to let it go? And how to truly let it go, and not allow the discomfort, annoyance, or even anger to poison our time with our loved ones, and our children's time with their grandparents?

Some conflicts, of course, are too deep-seated to be easily resolved or dismissed. Many, however, arise between people who truly love one another and want what is best for our children—but just have different visions (sometimes extremely different) of what that may be. In these cases, I believe that the Fifth Commandment—"Honor your father and your mother"—provides invaluable guidance.

Remember that this commandment does not expire when we reach adulthood, nor when we have children of our own. And also remember that our children are watching more than we know—and that the way we treat our parents serves as an early model for the way our little ones will treat us when they grow up and bring their own children— our grandchildren—over to play. This may help us give our parents and in-laws the benefit of the doubt, and make us feel better about stepping back, bending our own rules, and watching our children and their grandparents find their own way to one another, forging their own separate and special relationship. After all, we hope someday we will be the ones wanting to offer our precious grandchildren extra big slices of cake—and feeling that after all we did to rear our own children, we should certainly be allowed to do so.

But the Fifth Commandment will also help us realize when it is time to step in. When we feel genuinely dishonored as parents—when our authority is questioned or undercut in front of our children, for example, or when our standards for our children's health and safety are not upheld— we can and should intervene. Our duty to honor our own parents is sacred, and essential—but so is our children's obligation to honor us; and we cannot tolerate behavior that might encourage our little ones to treat us with disrespect or defiance. While speaking up is rarely easy, we may find the ensuing conversations—if conducted with discretion, mutual respect, and loving honesty—surprisingly helpful, and healing.

The Hebrew word for family, *mishpachah,* is one of the first our little ones will learn in religious school. The family has always been central to Jewish life, and when our relatives are scattered around the country—or even the globe—it falls to us to instill a sense of belonging, of community, of *mishpachah* in our children.

The task is not always easy, but hopefully it is almost always gratifying. Love, after all, is a powerful and transcendent thing; if, as we read in the Bible, love is stronger than death,[15] it is certainly far stronger than distance and the occasional quarrel or two. With mindfulness, devotion,

---

[15]Song of Songs 8:6.

creativity, patience, and understanding we can help our little ones feel the love of their extended families across the miles. And as ancestors we never knew did for their descendants they never met—and as our own grandparents and parents did for us—we too can bring the next generation into the warm embrace of *mishpachah*.

5

Teach Me Your Ways
Instilling Jewish Family Values

For my husband and me (and, I suspect, for many who came of age during the Bush/Quayle years), the phrase "family values" functioned best as a punch line—until we became parents. Then, suddenly, it wasn't so funny anymore. More than potty and pre-reading skills, our children needed values—strong, meaningful values to shape them into the people they were meant to be. They needed to learn what we believed, and why; what we did, and how; and what we—their family, their community, their religion, even their God—expected of them. And it was up to us to impart this knowledge. It was up to us—it *is* up to each of us—to instill in our little ones Jewish family values.

What exactly are Jewish family values? How can they help us rear our children? How can they help our little ones grow to their full potential? And how can we implant these values in our children when we ourselves may lack Jewish education, or may struggle with our faith, or may feel ambivalent about our relationship with the Divine?

As we know and experience each day, our children give us a precious chance to see everything anew, through their eyes. And they can teach us so much about how to approach the world—with wonder, with curiosity, and with tons of "whys?" If our little ones have a question, they don't reprimand themselves for not already knowing the answer or feel embarrassed about asking someone who does. They realize they have lots to learn, and they pack as many queries into a day as they possibly can. We too may feel we have a lot to learn. That's what rabbis, cantors, teachers, friends—even this book—are for. And that's what Judaism is for—taking our questions seriously and providing meaningful answers.

If we let them, our children also grant us an opportunity to renew our relationship with God and with the divine spark in each of us. Our children look with wonder at sunsets and snowfalls. They crunch leaves and smell flowers and follow ants. They fling their arms wide at the sheer beauty and enormity of God's creation. Though they may be too young to say it in words, they are not too young to feel it: They are loved, and cared for, and cherished. They are part of something great. And so are we.

King David said it three thousand years ago, and he said it beautifully: "Teach me Your ways, O Eternal One...for Your love is faithful and abundant!"[1] Jewish values teach our children—and us—about what they are part of. These values help us live the way we should live—the way we want to live. They guide us to respect the world around us, to embrace the divine potential within us. They enjoin us to seek and to share, to be thankful and to try our best. And always, they proclaim God's presence in our lives, and God's faithful and abundant love.

I Love You...and So Does God:
Helping Your Child Meet the Holy One

I want to share perhaps the best-kept secret in Judaism:

God loves you.

---

[1]Psalms 86:11, 13.

I grew up in a warm and loving Jewish home. I attended a highly regarded Jewish day school. I became bat mitzvah and was confirmed in a beautiful synagogue. But in all my Jewish childhood experiences—and they were many, and wonderful—I do not recall a single adult ever telling me "God loves you."

It's not surprising. After all, many Jews simply do not talk about God. We may grapple with God's role in our lives, or even with God's existence. We may have a hard time reconciling the image of an all-powerful, all-benevolent God with the suffering we witness in the world. We may see ourselves as too rational to take seriously the ancient notion of a Supreme Being. And we may feel uncomfortable, or inauthentic, or uncertain, sharing what we do believe about God.

Our ambivalence about God does not make us bad people. It doesn't even make us bad Jews. After all, our name—"Israel"—denotes "a people who struggles with God." But neither does our ambivalence negate these enduring truths: God lives. God loves us. God loves our children. And we—and our children—deserve to know it.

I believe that one of the greatest gifts we can give our children is the knowledge that God loves us. Instilling this value may not be easy—especially when it does not come naturally to us. But we can—and we should—teach our little ones about God's existence and God's love. And as we bring God to life for our children, we may find our own spirits stirring, recognizing and sensing the Divine presence in our world.

We can start small—very small. When putting our children to bed, we can simply add God to the list of those who love them: "I love you, and so does God. I love you, and God loves you." If we start this practice when our children are still infants or toddlers, they will grow up feeling as familiar with and secure in God's love as they do in our own. It really is that easy. When they get old enough to ask questions—"Who is God?" or "Why does God love me?"—offer brief, clear answers that they can relate to: "God created the world and all of us," "God brings the sun out in the morning and watches over us at night," "God made you special, and God loves you because you're you—just like I do!" Our children don't need fancy explanations or a theological discourse, especially if we aren't quite certain what we would say. They just need to feel that God is here, and that God cares.

In addition to talking *about* God, we can guide our children to talk *to* God. Even though our children may be small (compared to God and the whole of Creation, we're all pretty tiny), God yearns for them—and for us—to reach out, to share our thoughts and our feelings, our fears and our hopes. What better way to build our little ones' self-esteem than teaching them God wants to hear from them—and what better way to foster their relationship with God than helping them actually communicate with the Divine.

The sage Rav Ze'era taught: "A man may have a favorite who so importunes him with his needs and his wants that the man comes to dislike him and tries to avoid him. But with the Holy One, blessed be God, this is not so! The more a person importunes God with [her] needs and [her] wants, the more God loves [her]. So it is said, 'Call unto Me, and I will answer You.'"[2] By Rav Ze'era's standards, our little ones—persistent, unself-conscious, and always ready to express their needs and wants—are the ideal people to approach God. All we need is to encourage them to do so.

As we know, our children are great imitators. They will learn to speak regularly with God if they see us doing the same, and if we provide plenty of opportunities for them to follow our example. This means, of course, that we ourselves need to become comfortable talking to God.

If you don't know quite how to begin, or what to talk about, let Jewish tradition be your guide. There are two elements to Jewish worship: *keva*—the fixed, ordered prayers—and *kavanah*—the intention of the person praying, or what we might call the spiritual aspect of prayer. Although feeling a spiritual connection to God—experiencing the element of *kavanah*—may not come right away, it is easy enough to delve into the element of *keva*—to recite certain prayers at certain times. And the genius of Jewish worship is that *keva*—saying prayers—ultimately leads to *kavanah*—a spiritual awakening to our connection with God.

---

[2]*Midrash Tehillim* 4:3, in Bialik 524:170.

Even our most familiar prayers, prayers we might recite by rote, can bring us closer to God if we say them mindfully. Begin your meals with *HaMotzi*, explaining to your child, "Before we eat, we say thank you to God for giving us food." Just this sentence will teach your child so much: that God grants her sustenance, that she can approach God, and that God likes it when she says thank you. Chant the *Sh'ma* at bedtime, telling your child, "This prayer is our most special prayer. It means that there is only one God and that God will live forever." My sons' preschool teacher would invite her charges to "say good morning to God" before leading them in *Modeh Ani*,[3] the prayer for waking up, and the morning *Sh'ma*; it's a wonderful way to welcome the day at home as well.

As these practices come to feel more natural, you may find yourself looking for new occasions to evoke and thank God; fortunately, our prayer book is happy to oblige. The traditional morning blessings discussed in Chapter 2—called *Nisim Kol Yom*, or "Everyday Miracles"—provide an incredible framework for finding God's hand in our daily lives. Thanking God for nightfall and dawn, for the world's order and our body's function, for sight and strength and freedom, we come to understand that all we take for granted are truly divine gifts. Judaism also teaches us to offer a blessing on special occasions, even occasions we might not at first regard as particularly special: putting on new clothes, experiencing a thunderstorm, seeing a rainbow, even encountering a very smart person. Saying these blessings—and sharing them with your child—will help both of you become more attuned to God's active presence in our world. (You'll find the *Nisim Kol Yom* and blessings for special occasions in Appendix C.)

Over time you and your child will add your own words to the voices of our tradition. Let your child hear you praise God ("What a beautiful afternoon God made for us!"), thank God ("We're so grateful, God, for our wonderful vacation and our special time as a family"), implore God ("God, we feel so sick and sad. Please watch over us and help us get better soon"), and just talk to God ("Work was tough today. I'm going to tell

---

[3]*Modeh Ani* (or *Modah Ani* for girls) thanks God for restoring our bodies and souls after a night of sleep. The blessing can be found in Appendix C.

God about what happened, and that will help me feel better.") You need not compose magnificent acrostics or intricate praises (although why not, if you feel moved to do so)—you need simply to reach out to God, and trust God to reach back.

A Chasidic story tells of a little boy who was playing hide and seek with a friend. The little boy hid; but instead of looking for him, the friend ran off to play another game. When the little boy realized what had happened, he went crying to his grandfather, Rabbi Baruch. The rabbi began to cry as well, telling his grandson that such was God's experience: God, too, hides—and waits in vain to be sought.[4]

It is true that God hides. It is true that God can be hard to talk about, and hard to talk to, and hard to find. But it is also true that God is here, and that God longs to be sought, and found.

It is true that many Jews do not talk about the fact that God loves us. But it is also true that God does love us, and our little ones, and that God longs to be loved in return.

And It Was Very Good: Teaching Respect for God's Creations

According to the Book of Genesis, God ended the six days of Creation on a satisfied note: God beheld all that had been fashioned—from sand to stars, from beetle to buffalo—and proclaimed it "very good."[5]

Before granting Adam and Eve stewardship over the divine creation, our ancient Rabbis added, God charged them to treat the world with the care it deserved: "When the Holy One, blessed be God, created the first [human beings], God took [them] and led [them] round all the trees of the Garden of Eden, saying: 'Behold My works, how beautiful and praiseworthy they are! All that I have created, I created for your sake. Pay heed that you do not corrupt and destroy My universe—for if you do, there will be no one to repair it after you.'"[6]

---

[4]In Stern, *Gates of Repentance*, 230.
[5]Genesis 1:31.
[6]Ecclesiastes *Rabbah* 7:13.

Science has taught us—quite painfully—the truth of God's words. If we corrupt and destroy this universe, no one will repair it. If we treat God's creations with dishonor and disrespect, no one will revive them. Happily, the converse of this teaching is also true: If we safeguard and care for this universe, it will survive. If we treat God's creations with honor and respect, they will thrive.

We can call this Jewish value *shomrei adamah*—serving as guardians of the natural world. It is one of our highest values. And it is one of the easiest—and the most fun—to instill in our little ones.

Our children come into the world brimming with curiosity about and love for the world God created. No one else evinces as much interest in dirt and puddles, bugs and squirrels, shapes in the clouds and piles of colorful leaves. No one else expresses such excitement about stroking a soft pet, watching fish swim in lazy, endless circles, or happening upon a dog squatting to go poop. No one else more devotedly kicks off their shoes to feel the sand or mud against their feet, or lifts their heads to feel the wind or rain upon their faces.

Because our children are so attuned to the natural world, we will find plenty of opportunities to explain Who created these wonders, and introduce the idea that we bear responsibility for taking care of them. Most little ones will be delighted to feel that they can help care for something so much bigger than they are, and will eagerly respond when asked to do so. Put your child in charge of tossing the newspaper into the recycling bin or switching off the lights when he leaves a room, or have him scoop the dog's kibble, or ask him to touch the soil of your houseplants and let you know which ones need to be watered. When you go to the park, challenge your child to throw away five pieces of litter (keep a supply of hand sanitizer with you) before he starts to play, or find a dog he thinks needs some petting (always accompany him, of course, and always ask the dog's owner first). Enthusiastically recognize all of these efforts: "When you put the paper in the recycling bin and turned off the light we weren't using, you helped save trees and energy," or "God created such wonderful plants and animals. Thanks for helping to keep them healthy and happy," or "You are really taking care of this beautiful world. Picking up trash helps keep it clean." Not only will our children learn good habits, but they will also feel tremendously empowered and important.

If we begin instilling this value of *shomrei adamah* when our children are very young, they will become accustomed to enjoying nature in a way that demonstrates reverence for God's creations. Teach your child not to pull at flowers or yank leaves off of trees by saying something like, "Look at those bright yellow sunflowers! Let's smell them and touch them very gently. We won't pick them, though, because then they won't be able to grow bigger and even more beautiful." Don't allow your child to chase birds, bat at trees, plants or flowers, stomp on bugs, or handle pets in a rough or unkind manner; and have a stock phrase you use to remind her why—perhaps something along the lines of "We treat the world with respect, and that means being gentle and kind to animals and plants." To teach this value fully, we may need to alter some of our own behavior; after all, it's hard to teach our little ones that they shouldn't smush ants if they see us chase down and kill a cockroach with a triumphant "gotcha!" As our Sages remind us: "Even those things you may hold superfluous in the world—such as fleas, gnats, and flies—even they are a part of the creation of the world. God carries out [the divine] purpose through everything—even through a gnat, even through a frog."[7]

Although Judaism rightfully emphasizes the importance of caring for the natural world in its entirety, we concern ourselves especially with the "climax of creation"—human beings.[8] After all, it was only after creating people that God's opinion of the divine work was elevated from merely "good" to "very good." And while teaching a child to embrace the different sizes and colors and forms in which human beings come may be harder than encouraging him to feed the hamster and water the plants, this too is an essential element of demonstrating respect for all of God's creations.

The Talmud records a beautiful story about the origin of humanity. While the Book of Genesis states only that God created people from "the dust of the earth,"[9] our Sages explain that God gathered dust of every

---

[7]Genesis *Rabbah* 10:7, in Klagsbrun, 458.
[8]Genesis *Rabbah* 14:1, in Bialik 14:57.
[9]Genesis 2:7.

color, from every corner of the earth, and mixed them all together to form the first human being.[10] It doesn't matter what we look like or where we come from; we are all descended from the same ancestor, all equal in the eyes of God.

The lesson is an essential one to instill in our children, especially when—as they grow up—they will encounter a society that all too frequently fails to embrace this value. If we can teach our little ones to focus on a person's character—rather than his or her color, ethnicity, class, or physical appearance—we can guide them truly to honor God's greatest creations.

We can start while our children are still small. Purchase some dolls, figurines, and storybooks that depict people of other races, ethnicities, and family structures. And simply choosing our words carefully can emphasize so much. Rather than referring to workers as "garbagemen" or "the air-conditioning guys," we can call them "the gentlemen who collect the garbage" or "the people who fix the air conditioning." We can teach our little ones not to call housekeepers or adult babysitters by their first names, but to use the same honorifics they employ when addressing their teachers. And we can guard our own tongues; while conversation that reflects racism, homophobia, or the like hopefully does not take place in our home, our children are still listening—and learning—every time they hear us complain that we look so disgustingly fat.

Living by this value can bring some tough moments. Prejudice and stereotypes are—tragically—an endemic part of our society. It is far easier to smile uneasily when someone makes a derogatory remark than to say, "I don't agree with that" or "That kind of talk makes me uncomfortable"—but deep down we know the right thing to do. When we hear others impugn an entire religious group based on the actions of a few, or speak cruelly of another person because he or she is overweight, or joke about someone's sexual orientation, we owe it to our children, to God's creations, and to ourselves to speak up.

As our little ones grow older, they will have questions: Why is that man a different color than I am? Why is that lady's voice so hard to un-

---

[10]*Sanhedrin* 38b, in Bialik 14:50.

derstand? Why is that person sitting in a wheelchair? Why is that lady bald? Why is that man so wrinkly? Why is that person so fat? So curious about their surroundings, and so happily unaware of the loaded nature of their inquiries, our children don't mean any harm; they just want to understand how people of such varied shapes, colors, sizes, ages, and appearances fit together in the world.

Not everyone, of course, will be so charmed by our children's thirst for knowledge. If people overhear your little one's posing a possibly upsetting query, make sure they also hear you answer in a way that demonstrates respect and kindness for all. First, apologize for your child (of course she didn't mean anything by it, but if someone was made to feel embarrassed or sad, an "I'm sorry" is still in order), then tell her, "God made us in many different ways, and each of us is special," and add that you'll talk about it more when the two of you are alone. Later, explain that she can always ask you anything, but that if she has a question about someone else, she must say it quietly so as not to hurt anyone's feelings.

Your child may also notice that some of his friends have only one parent, or two parents of the same gender. The younger your little one is, the better to introduce him matter-of-factly to the various shapes a family can take. "God makes all families different. Some families have only one mom or one dad. Some families have a mom and a dad. Some families have two moms or two dads. There are all kinds of different families, and every family is special."

These conversations can also help your little one acknowledge same-sex relationships as unquestioningly as she does mixed-gender relationships. Not only is this a great gift for your child, but also a great gift for those who strive to create loving families in a society too often filled with homophobia and hatred. If your little one asks why her friend has two moms and no dad, for example, say: "You know how Jorgito has a mom and a dad? God made Jorgito's mom the kind of lady who wants to marry a man and have children with a man. And God made Jorgito's dad the kind of man who wants to marry a lady and have children with a lady. So Jorgito has one mom and one dad. And you know how Maddie has two moms? God made Maddie's moms the kind of ladies who want to marry a lady and have children with a lady. So Maddie has no dad but two moms." We may be amazed at how easily our little ones accept this explanation. (My daughter, in particular, took it to heart; a few weeks after we had a conversation about her friend Evan and his same-gender parents, she got upset when I reprimanded her for disobeying me. "Your job is to listen to Mommy," I told her, to which she replied, "Evan has two daddies!")

"All that I have created," God tells humanity, "I created for your sake." Living in God's glorious world, surrounded by God's glorious creations, is a great privilege, and a great responsibility. We are charged with caring for the plants and the animals, the sea and the sky—and for one another. And—most importantly—we are charged with rearing the next generation of guardians for nature and for humanity.

Looking at our little ones—playing in the dirt, watching birds fly overhead, throwing stray gum wrappers away—it is perhaps not so difficult to imagine them one day fulfilling this role. And if we instill in our children the values of *shomrei adamah*, and respect for all people, they will indeed become the worthy caretakers God seeks.

Who Is Rich?: Being Satisfied With What You Have

Kohelet—the speaker in the Book of Ecclesiastes—knew what he was talking about: "The eye never has enough of seeing, nor the ear enough of hearing...a lover of money never has his fill of money, nor a lover of wealth his fill of income."[11] And this was in the days before stocks and iPhones, Chicken Dance Elmo, and Disney Princess!

We feel the truth of *Kohelet*. Even when we have what we need, we still want more. And our children feel it, too. One of their first words, after all, is not "less" or "plenty"—it's "more."

---

[11] Ecclesiastes 1:8, 5:9.

The problem with wanting more, of course, is that we never feel we have enough—by definition, there's always more to get. And we may be so busy looking for more that we forget to enjoy what we already have.

Just ask our little ones. One night after dinner I handed my son a dish of pudding for dessert. Instead of saying thank you and digging in, he started inspecting his serving, comparing it to what I'd doled out to his brother and sister. Was his bigger, he wanted to know, or smaller? They were all the same. If he finished his pudding, would he get more? Or if he wanted some chocolate chips put on top, would he get some? What happened next was such a cliché but it's true—he spent so much time trying to angle for more pudding that bedtime came and he didn't even get to finish what he'd had in the first place. (No, that wasn't a fun night.)

No matter what sort of treat we're offering, the situation often comes down to the same thing: Our children want more. And when the desire for more is too strong, it hurts everyone. It hurts our little ones because they aren't taking pleasure in what they have already. And it hurts us because we feel unappreciated and inadequate.

No wonder that the ancient sage Ben Zoma taught: "Who is rich? Those who find happiness in their portion."[12] That is exactly what we want to be, exactly what we want to instill in our children. But how? When our children instinctively seem to clamor for more, how can we help them "find happiness in their portion"?

It may seem counterintuitive, but I think the best way to enable children to find happiness in what they have is to give them less. If you've spent the day at the zoo, skip the gift shop. If you're going out for ice cream, skip the topping. If your child goes crazy for a toy at a friend's house or preschool, don't run out and buy it. If a tchotchke catches his eye at the store, agree that it looks pretty cool—but don't add it to your cart. If you're planning his birthday party, acknowledge that renting a petting zoo and bounce house would make a memorable gathering—but keep the celebration simple and restrained. Our job, after all, is not to give our

---

[12]*Pirkei Avot* 4:1.

children everything they want, but to teach them to enjoy what they have. And if they're always getting something new, the "getting"—rather than the "having" and the "enjoying"—becomes the focus.

If you explain this to your child, you may find her surprisingly receptive. Even more than feeling indulged, children like to feel included—and if you present this value as something you think is important and want to share with her, she will. Before heading to the ice cream store, you can say: "I'm so excited to take you out for ice cream! You can pick any flavor you like; but we won't be getting any toppings, because just going out for ice cream is enough of a treat." This phrase can actually become sort of a mantra: "We've had so much fun at the zoo! As soon as we finish feeding the ducks, it will be time to go home. We won't be buying anything at the gift shop, because going to the zoo is enough of a treat." Over time your little one will grow accustomed to hearing this, and even come to understand and embrace it.

But not always, of course, and not right away. Particularly if our little ones are used to getting most if not all of what they ask for, making the transition to "finding happiness in [their] portion[s]" will take some work. But a few outbursts and some whining are, in the long run, a small price to pay for instilling this value.

First, make sure you're not pulling the rug out from under your little one. Don't wait till you get to the toy aisle at the supermarket, and his eyes are darting from possibility to possibility, to announce that you won't be buying anything. Prepare him in advance: "I know when we go shopping, you usually get a toy. But we've been buying a lot of toys lately, and I want you to enjoy playing with those instead of always getting something new. So we won't be buying a new toy today." Let him fuss and complain for a few minutes—we'd be disappointed, too!—but stand firm. Just before heading into the store, tell him: "I know you're sad we won't be buying a new toy today. But if you do a good job cooperating while we shop, we'll be able to read an extra story when we get home." Replacing the acquisition of a new toy with the promise of some special time together underscores what is truly important, and what you want to give to your child.

Once you've explained to your child what is going to happen, she will know what to expect. She may not like it, however—and she may make her displeasure known publicly and loudly. Here's an example: Say you've brought her to the ice cream parlor, she's asked for a topping, and you've cheerfully reminded her that ice cream is enough of a treat. But when you give her the dish of ice cream, instead of saying "thank you," she starts hollering that she wants a topping. What to do now? Try immediately taking away the ice cream, taking her out of the ice cream store, and telling her that she has a choice. You will count to ten. When you reach ten, she can apologize for yelling at you and say thank you for the ice cream, and then you will give her the ice cream. Or she can choose not to apologize and not to say thank you, and you will throw the ice cream away. Then follow through. If you end up throwing the ice cream away and packing her into the car while she screams hysterically, you will probably feel horrible. (Believe me, I know.) It's awful to see what was supposed to be a fun outing turn into a total disaster. But in the long run, you really are giving your child a great gift. You are teaching her that she cannot have everything she wants, and that she needs to express appreciation for what she has. And the next time you take her for ice cream, she will probably remember to say thank you for the scoop.

This is only one approach and won't necessarily be right for every family and every child. Let me clarify that I don't think it's wrong for our children to want things, and to tell us that they want them. And I don't think it's our job to discourage them from wanting things. It doesn't make sense to tell a little one, "You have a truck just like that one at home. You don't need that truck." You may not think he needs that truck, but he thinks he does—and the distinction between need and want is pretty much lost on a toddler or preschooler anyway.

What we can do, however, is help our little ones learn that they can't have everything they want, and help them enjoy what they have. Tell your child instead, "That's a neat truck, isn't it? We won't buy it, but you have one like it already. Let's play with it when we get home." And make sure you do. After all, your empathy and your attention are the "portion" your child craves most of all.

Grant Me the Ability to Be Alone:
Fostering Self-Reliance and Independence

It is the irony of parenting: Our ultimate job is to put ourselves out of a job. We take care of our children in order to teach them to take care of themselves.

And while no toddler or preschooler is ready to tackle life (or even breakfast!) on her own, our little ones may be more capable than we realize—or than we are willing to admit. It is so tempting to do everything we can for our children—it's faster, for one thing (as anyone who has waited for a two-year-old to fix her hair "all by myself!" can attest), and it can feel like the right thing to do. But when we give our little ones some space and some responsibility, they may astound us—and delight themselves—with what they can accomplish.

The Chasidic Rabbi Nachman of Bratslav would pray to God: "Sovereign of the Universe, grant me the ability to be alone." What an elemental skill is the ability to be alone: to rely on ourselves, to enjoy our own company, to feel confident and competent and secure and safe. And what a great gift it is to give our children.

Of course our little ones need to be with us. And in addition to feeding, sheltering, and dressing them, we want to share plenty of fun time— playing, reading, snuggling, exploring, and just enjoying being together. Our children delight in our attention, and in our interactions with them. We help our little ones realize themselves and their potential.

And yet, even for toddlers, there is such a thing as too much togetherness. When they pick up a toy, and we immediately demonstrate its use or quiz them on its colors, they lose the chance to discover and learn for themselves. When they scribble their fifth picture of blue swirls and yellow lines, and we erupt in praise, they miss the opportunity to consider and evaluate their own work. And when they occupy themselves happily, but we insert ourselves into their play, they cannot nurture the ability to be alone.

When our little ones seek us out, wanting us to help them, play with them, cheer for them, and simply be with them, we'd like to say yes as often as we can. But perhaps we should not say yes every time. Instead of sitting and watching them do a puzzle, clapping when they insert a piece correctly and jumping in when they don't, we can say, "That puzzle looks like fun. I'll read my book over here while you work on it, and in a few minutes you can show me how it's coming." Instead of applauding even their most lackluster efforts at cleanup, we can prompt, "Do you think that is really the best job you can do?" Instead of rushing to assist when they have trouble getting their shoes on the right feet, we can empathize, "It's tough putting on shoes all by yourself! Keep trying; you'll get it." And instead of joining them on the floor when we see them absorbed in their toys, we can smile to ourselves at how cute and busy they are—and leave them alone.

Only when our children are left alone will they develop the ability to be alone. Only when they have the space to begin learning self-reliance will they become self-reliant. And only when they have the opportunity to get to know themselves will they learn, and trust in, who they are and who they are becoming.

This process is an essential one, even a sacred one—and though it centers on our children's needs, it requires plenty of patience and wisdom on our part. Is there anything, after all, that takes longer than a child doing whatever-it-is "all by myself"? While our little ones' aptitude probably lags far behind their enthusiasm, it's so important for us to encourage these impulses of going it alone. Whether it's trying to pull on their own clothes, climb into the car seat, figure out a toy, or "help" around the house, our children need time and space to learn what they are capable of, and to challenge themselves. They also need an atmosphere that supports their efforts: healthful snacks on shelves they can reach, at least one pair of slip-on or Velcro-fastened shoes, unbreakable dishes so they can practice setting and clearing their places (and maybe ours, too) at the table. And, most of all, they need us to step back and let them begin to do for themselves.

Of course it can't be like this all day every day. There will be times that we have to step in and take over—especially when we have somewhere to go, or something to do, and the task for which we allotted two minutes is stretching into ten—but even then we can do so gently: "You are really working hard at making your bed! You did so well pulling up the sheet. It's almost time to leave so I'm going to help you with your quilt, and tomorrow you can try again all by yourself." If your little one wants to attempt something that is truly beyond his ability, see if you can simplify the job but still give him a chance to succeed: Rather than letting him pour milk from a newly-opened carton, for example, fill up a small plastic pitcher that he can use instead. But don't be afraid to say no when you need to: There is just no way to accommodate a preschooler's desire to use a saw, or put something in the oven, or cross the street by himself, and being taught such boundaries will help him understand his place and his limitations.

Watching our little ones take even the smallest steps toward independence—and away from us—brings such bittersweet feelings. We celebrate their growing up, but we still yearn to hold them close. We want them to learn and develop and do, but maybe not so much, and maybe not quite yet. But this is, after all, the job we signed on for. It is our children's job to become self-reliant, and it is our job to let them.

Rabbi Nachman's prayer, then, resonates with both parents and children: the children struggling to do it "all by myself," and the parents struggling to let them, the children learning to feel complete on their own, and the parents learning to let them do so. "Sovereign of the Universe, grant me the ability to be alone."

Tzedakah: Generosity and Justice

Any discussion of Jewish family values must include *tzedakah*. *Tzedakah* stands as one of Judaism's key mitzvot, one of our greatest obligations as Jews—and as human beings. The word is often translated as "charity," but it actually means "justice." While generosity and giving are important components of *tzedakah*, it is more than that. *Tzedakah* is doing right by those who are in need. *Tzedakah* is, truly, a way of life.

And these early years of our little ones' lives are a wonderful time to begin instilling the value of *tzedakah*. Despite the stereotype of young children as totally self-absorbed beings, we know that our children are capable of great empathy. When they hear a playmate crying, they rush to see what is wrong or begin to cry as well; when they see us looking sad, they offer a hug or take our hand. We also know that our little ones want to help, and contribute, and feel a part of things. Practicing the mitzvah of *tzedakah* enables them to engage these impulses, and to set out on a most praiseworthy way of life.

Our little ones, of course, learn best when they have our example to follow. Make *tzedakah* a familiar act in your home; have your child decorate a cardboard box to keep in the pantry, then encourage her to help you pick out a can or two of nonperishable food to be donated to a local food bank every time she accompanies you to the grocery store. She—and you—will delight in seeing the box slowly fill up. You might also display a *tzedakah* box on a low shelf (you can buy beautiful *tzedakah* boxes at Judaica and synagogue gift shops, or help your child make one out of a coffee can, shoebox, or even a paper towel roll) and drop a few coins in it every day or as part of your family Shabbat rituals. Let your little one put in coins as well (this is also a great way to teach her to recognize pennies, nickels, dimes, and quarters) and thank her for helping you do *tzedakah*. As you perform these acts of *tzedakah*, explain to your child: "God has given us so much, and it's our job to share with people who don't have enough. When these boxes are full, we'll make sure they get to people who need help." When you are ready to empty the food or *tzedakah* box, your child can help you carry cans to the car or sort and roll coins, then come along when you drop off your donations at a local agency. If you call in advance to let them know you and your little one are bringing a contribution, someone may be willing to meet with you briefly and give you and your little one a personal thanks. It will make your child—and you—feel great about giving.

Tzedakah can become a regular part of your family's celebrations as well. When your little one is listing gifts he hopes to receive for his birthday, have him add a few items a disadvantaged child might like; purchase these along with his presents, then bring them to an agency after the festivities. Most Jewish holidays have a built-in *tzedakah* component; many synagogues sponsor food drives around Rosh Hashanah and Yom

Kippur, and we are expressly commanded to remember the needy during Sukkot, Purim, Passover, and Shavuot. These can be wonderful times for engaging with your child in acts of *tzedakah*—from donating some of his gently used toys and clothing to making and delivering cards for nursing home residents. In order to combat the materialism so often associated with Chanukah, one of my friends invented Mitzvah Madness for her family; rather than anticipating a different gift each night, her children plan eight days of different *tzedakah* projects.

While most of these experiences will be enjoyable for your child, be sure she understands their significance as more than just a fun outing: "It's so important for us to help people who need help. When we give clothes and food to people who don't have enough clothes to wear or food to eat, we're doing *tzedakah*. God is so proud of us for doing the right thing, and I'm proud of us, too," or "The people who live in this nursing home might be feeling lonely because their families aren't with them right now. I know these cards you made will help them feel happy and cared for. You are really doing a good thing." Over time little ones will come to understand and instinctively accept their responsibility for caring for those who have less, for reaching out to those in need.

As essential as the element of giving is, *tzedakah* comprises even more than generosity. *Tzedakah* does, after all, mean justice. And pursuing justice is a central obligation of Judaism.

The Torah delineates 613 commandments for us to follow. Of all these commandments, one is repeated significantly more than any other: the charge to care for the stranger, "for you were strangers in the land of Egypt."[13] Remembering our terrible sufferings as strangers in Egypt, we resolve to help the strangers in our midst. Recalling the injustice visited upon us, we seek justice for them.

Who are these strangers, and how do we help ensure that they are treated justly? There are so many answers to these questions. The strangers may be the working poor, or single parents, or immigrants struggling to prosper—or even to survive—economically. The strangers may be

---

[13]Leviticus 19:34, among others.

peaceable members of religious or ethnic groups unfairly castigated for the deeds of others. The strangers may be fighting or fleeing for their lives in faraway lands, persecuted for their beliefs, their gender, the shade of their skin, or the region of their birth.

We are so limited in what we can do. But for the sake of *tzedakah*—and the sake of our children—we must do what we can. Explain to your little one in simple language what injustice you are trying to ameliorate, and what you are doing: "I read in the newspaper about a woman who works really hard but can't make enough money to buy all the food she needs. I'm going to write a letter to the people who are in charge and tell them I think that's wrong. Would you like to help me find paper and a pen to write the letter?" or "I'm so upset that in another country people are hurting each other just because their skin is a different color. There's a big meeting of people who think that's wrong, and we're going to go. We'll be singing songs and waving signs about how important it is to stop the fighting." Not only will you be making a difference, you will be teaching your child to make a difference as well. Not only will you practice the deepest meaning of *tzedakah*, you will instill this value in your child as well.

Over time your little one will learn to apply this aspect of *tzedakah*—the aspect of justice—to his own experiences. Help your child find examples of injustice in storybooks or television shows and talk about them. My middle son used to go into paroxysms of outrage over *The Little Mermaid*, demanding to know how Ariel could fall in love with Prince Eric when all she knew about him was that he was handsome, and why Ariel had to become a human at the end instead of Eric's becoming a merman. Encourage your child to be welcoming to new children, to comfort a sad child, or to tell a bullying child "Stop it!" If our children learn now that they have the power—and the responsibility—to recognize and work against injustice, they will carry the lesson—and the inspiration to act—with them throughout their lives.

The Sage Rabbi Tarfon taught: "You are not required to complete the work, but neither are you at liberty to abstain from it."[14] We know—and

---

[14]*Pirkei Avot* 2:21.

our children will discover too soon—that we cannot save the whole world with our acts of *tzedakah*. No matter how sincere our intentions, how fervent our practice, how strong our will, there is much we cannot do, and many we cannot help. But knowing this does not negate our obligation to do the good—and to help the people—that we can.

Our children will learn quickly that life is not fair. When we instill in them the importance of *tzedakah*, however, their attention will come to focus less on the imagined injustice of an early bedtime and more on the injustice facing those who are truly in need. Teaching our little ones about *tzedakah*—about generosity and justice—teaches them how to assist and how to act.

6

A Stiff-Necked People
Challenges and Discipline

✍

Each year at Passover, the Haggadah enjoins us to remember the Exodus from Egypt as if we experienced it ourselves. Rather than saying "God brought *our ancestors* out of Egypt," we recite: "God brought *us* out of Egypt, divided the Red Sea for *us*, [and] sustained *us* for forty years in the desert."[1]

The practice is a powerful and moving one. In replacing "they" with "we," we identify with our forbearers. We imagine ourselves in their places, as the recipients of God's greatest miracles and greatest goodness.

Yet all was not perfect in the wilderness. We found ourselves in a new and challenging place; God was with us, but we sometimes felt alone and afraid. We grappled with our newfound freedom, trying to determine our capacities and our limitations. And although we knew God and Moses devoted themselves to our care, still we lashed out at them, too often treating them with disrespect and unkindness.

God and Moses grew impatient—even angry—with us. They called us a "stiff-necked people"[2]—stubbornly doing the wrong thing even when we knew better, testing to be certain their love was unconditional, acting out because we did not know how else to cope with the conflicted and complicated feelings raging inside us.

But God and Moses did not give up on us, nor on themselves. They continued to teach us and to guide us. They continued to love us and to

---

[1] Bronstein, 53.
[2] Exodus 32:9.

lead us. The journey was not easy for us, nor for them; but together, we came to the place we were meant to be.

We reenact this drama in every generation. And yes, it is we parents who play the roles of God and Moses, and our children who portray the stiff-necked people—stubbornly doing the wrong thing even when they know better, testing to be certain our love is unconditional, acting out because they do not know how else to cope with the conflicted and complicated feelings raging inside them.

These toddler and preschool years are magical years. But they are also difficult years—for us and for our children. As our children delight in all they can do, they also grow fearful of getting too big, of losing the protection and security of babyhood. As our children begin to enjoy their increased privileges, they also begin to resent their boundaries. And as our children draw near to us in love and affection, they also lash out against us in frustration and anger.

We can't expect our little ones effortlessly to navigate all of these emotions, any more than God and Moses expected perfection from us in the wilderness. Our children have a right to their resentment, to their frustration, even to their anger. They have a right to express these feelings, and to be heard.

But with *their* right comes *our* responsibility. We have a responsibility to teach our children how to manage these emotions. We have a responsibility to teach our children to express these feelings in acceptable ways. And we have a responsibility to bring our children through these turbulent years so they can become the people they are meant to be.

These toddler and preschool years will put us to the test. Our children will hit us when we are with them and scream when we are not. They will whine and bite. They will throw toys and refuse to sleep. They will do this without regard for where they are, or for who is watching.

They will do this because they are struggling to tell us something, and they do not know how else to express themselves. They will do this to find out if our love has conditions or limits. They will do this to see if we will let them get away with it. They will do this unless and until we teach them a better way.

And there is, indeed, a better way.

Know Before Whom You Stand: A Philosophy of Discipline

In order to teach our little ones a better way, we must have their respect.

When our children are infants, we work so hard to demonstrate our love, our care, our ceaseless concern. Everything we do focuses on them, on their needs, on their wants. We give all that we can; we demand nothing in return.

This is the way it should be when our little ones are babies. But too often this is the way things are even when our little ones become toddlers and preschoolers.

As our children grow, our relationship with them needs to change. We still give, of course; but we must demand something in return. We must demand respect.

On his deathbed, Rabbi Eliezer charged his students: "When you pray, know before Whom you stand."[3] We feel free to pour out our feelings before God, aware that God knows our best and our worst. We feel secure in God's unconditional love. But we also remember Who God is. We stand before God with honor. We conduct ourselves with respect.

Our children must learn before whom they stand. We are their parents. They should feel free to pour out their feelings before us, aware that we know their best and their worst. They should feel secure in our unconditional love. But they must also remember who we are. They should stand before us with honor. They should conduct themselves with respect.

Like so many other values, respectfulness originates with us. Too often we fail to command our children's respect. We want to be their friends. We don't want to intimidate them. We want them to like us. We don't want to stunt their natural spirit.

---

[3]*B'rachot* 28b.

These impulses have some merit. But the need to earn our children's respect will often conflict with—and even trump—the impulses. That our children respect us as their parents is essential. That we understand ourselves as worthy of demanding that respect is paramount.

But how do we instill this respectfulness in our children? We do this by remembering our role as parents, and making sure that our children remember it, too; by matter-of-factly teaching our children the rules, and what will happen if they follow the rules—or break them; by consistently enforcing logical and reasonable consequences for good and bad behavior; and by loving our children enough to be the boss.

Sounds great, doesn't it? But how do we put these appealing platitudes into practice?

Throughout this chapter, we will apply these principles to specific situations. For now, however, let me explain how they fit into a greater philosophy of discipline, and how this philosophy of discipline can guide us—and our children—through the joys and the challenges of the toddler and preschool years.[4]

First, we must understand discipline in a positive way—both philosophically and practically. While many parents today ascribe negative connotations to the term—using it interchangeably with "punishment"—Judaism actually views discipline as one of a parent's most exalted responsibilities, and as a reflection of God's love for humanity. "The one whom God loves, God corrects," explains the Book of Proverbs, "just as parents [correct] the children in whom they delight."[5] Our ancient Rabbis even charged parents who refrained from disciplining their children with "deprivation," according to author Miriam Levi. "Discipline is necessary for the child," she points out. "He [or she] has a right to it!"[6]

---

[4] I have benefited from the wisdom of Judaism, the wisdom of social science, and the wisdom of everyday experience in developing a philosophy of discipline. I am grateful to so many family members, friends, teachers, and experts in parenting and education who have—knowingly or not—influenced me with their ideas, insights, and practices. I want to cite especially the groundbreaking work of Lee and Marlene Canter, whose multiple books on Assertive Discipline have served me so well in my teaching and in my parenting.

[5] Proverbs 3:12.

[6] Levi, 82.

So what does it mean to discipline Jewishly? It means that when our children behave in a certain way, they will evoke consistent and foreseeable consequences—consequences they will like for good behavior, consequences they will not like for bad behavior. And the ultimate goal of discipline is to guide our children to make the right choice, to choose the good.

Discipline is truly a great gift for our children. It teaches them about the power of their actions, and their ability to control (to some degree) their own destiny. It teaches them that there are consequences to what they do. And it teaches them that they can count on us to react in appropriate and predictable ways when they do the right thing—or the wrong one.

These, of course, are long-term benefits. But even in our daily lives, discipline can be a very positive experience for our children—and for us. Rather than focusing on instances of misbehavior with lots of disapproving "no's," a system of discipline should actually center as much as possible on the good—on praising our little ones, on offering lots of "controlled choices" (more on this in a moment), and on, surprisingly, saying no as infrequently as possible.

Let's talk about these elements in more detail.

Our little ones probably make a lot more good choices than bad choices. The problem is we may tend not to notice the good choices. If they play nicely with a toy, or color on the paper rather than on the table, or open their mouths wide for tooth-brushing, we may take it for granted, and—since they are not at the moment demanding it—focus our attention elsewhere. It's just when the misbehavior starts that our attention flips back to them, now in a negative rather than a positive way.

According to Jewish tradition, this pattern is at least three thousand years old. In their commentary on the Book of Psalms, our Sages acclaim King David for his devotion to God; and they especially marvel that he reached out to God not only in times of tumult, but even when life was unfolding calmly and peacefully.[7] Apparently taking the good for granted was as common in ancient times as in our own.

---

[7]*Midrash Tehillim* 139:2, in Siegel, 199.

We can learn from King David's mindfulness; and we will find tremendous reward in reaching out to our children not only in times of tumult, but even when life is unfolding relatively calmly and peacefully. Acknowledging our children's good behavior goes so far in teaching them how to behave properly—and actually makes them want to do so. It's fun for parents, too. All we need to do is watch our little ones and give them positive reinforcement for doing the right thing. If they use a spoon instead of digging their fingers into the cereal bowl, we can beam and say, "You are using your spoon so well. What good manners!" If they respond quickly when called, we can tell them, "What good listening! You came as soon as I called you." If they're playing quietly while we tend to other tasks, we can take a moment to share our appreciation: "You're playing so nicely while I get my work done. It's great having you nearby." Because we may not be accustomed to speaking this way, or to commenting on so many relatively minor actions, this kind of talk may feel stilted or false at first. But soon enough it will come to sound—and feel—quite natural. And our little ones will take notice too; when they realize they can earn our praise and attention with positive behavior, they will choose positive behavior more often.

Speaking of choosing, we have all realized by now how much our children love to make their own choices. Unfortunately, many of their choices aren't appropriate ones—to eat a cookie for dinner, for example, or to check out twenty library books at a time. Within a system of discipline, however, our children can actually enjoy many opportunities to choose. The key is to offer "controlled choices"—to let them select something we have already approved. "Would you like Goldfish or a banana for snack?" we can ask. "Do you want to put away your book or your puzzle first?" "Do you want to wear your red sweater or your yellow one?" No matter which option our children pick, the end result is the same: an easy, healthful meal, a clean(er) room, a warm outfit. But when our little ones have some say in the matter—when they feel empowered to choose—they cooperate more, and resent less the times another will (usually ours) is imposed upon them.

Finally, a system of discipline should enable us to say "yes" much more often than "no." "No" should be a powerful word, but it loses its potency when our little ones hear it again and again. When we save "no" for the big moments, it will have more meaning—and it will make the rest of our day much more pleasant. My friends and I have actually made a little game out of this; I realize it sounds silly, but you'll be surprised how addictive it is. Try to come up with ways of saying no without actually using the word. Instead of "No running," for example, say "Please walk." Replace "No yelling" with "Please use your quiet voice," and "No video until you put away your toys" with "As soon as you clean up, I'll turn on the video." The instruction is the same, but the delivery is much more pleasant—and much more likely to inspire cooperation.

We can apply this technique to virtually any situation. When your little one is approaching the stove, checking you out over her shoulder to see if you're planning to intervene, walk over, take her hand, and say: "Let's move away from that hot stove and find your crayons." When your child asks to play outside but it's pouring rain, smile and answer, "That sounds fun; let's do it tomorrow!" When she wants a cookie, tell her, "I'll get one for you after dinner." Without saying no, we are able to achieve our goal—keeping our little ones safe, dry, and healthy—in an equally effective, much more positive way.

When we feel confident in our ability to manage our children's behavior, we will also be more likely to indulge their reasonable if not convenient requests. If your little one asks to paint, but you're exhausted after an afternoon of being hit and whined at, you're probably going to say no rather than deal with wrestling him into a smock, covering the table with newspaper, finding the art supplies, and supervising the clean-up. But if your system of discipline has helped him choose (mostly) good behavior, you'll probably have enough patience—and enough energy—to say yes. If your little one asks to jump on the bed, but you dread the screaming tantrum that inevitably follows your "time to stop!" directive, you'll probably just say no. But if your system of discipline has helped him understand that "time to stop" means exactly that, you'll probably say yes. These "yeses" are good for our little ones—and they're good for us.

Once our children understand that they can earn our attention through good behavior, once they feel empowered through making their own controlled choices, and once they hear more "yes" than "no," they will be less inclined to disobey and act out. However, even the most positive system of discipline will not eliminate all traces of misbehavior; our kids are kids, after all. Just as important as recognizing good behavior and encouraging good choices is responding to bad behavior and discouraging bad choices. In order to succeed, our system of discipline must enable us to do both effectively.

This second element of our system of discipline may not be as much fun—or as popular with our little ones—as the first, but it is essential. It does not negate the fact that we love our children unconditionally. It does not negate the fact that even when they talk back, or hit, or throw toys, we still love our children. But it does teach that loving and accepting our children does not mean that we love and accept their bad behavior. It does teach that our children are subject to rules they did not make and may not like—but that they must obey nonetheless.

And though our children may not realize it right away, this second element of discipline will benefit them tremendously. For this element is the key to helping our little ones learn their place—their place in the family, and their place in the world. It teaches our children that we have expectations, and standards, and rules we will require them to follow. It teaches our children that we believe in them, and want to help them succeed in choosing the good. And it teaches our children that no matter how much they may act as if they want to be in charge, we know that deep down, what they really need is to know that we love and care for them enough to be the boss.

In order to impart effectively all of these lessons, we truly must be willing to "be the boss." That means doing things that will at times make our little ones unhappy, frustrated, even angry; it means standing up to our children's crestfallen faces, disappointed tears, even cutting words. It means believing in ourselves, and in our ultimate responsibility to set our children on the right path; it means keeping faith with the writer of the Book of Proverbs, who assures us: "Discipline your [children] and [they] will give you peace...for happy is the one who heeds instruction."[8] Most of all, it means acting like an adult. It means being a parent.

Before moving on to the next section, I want to take just a moment to impress how essential acting like an adult and being a parent truly are. If you are blessed to have a spouse, you have an amazing opportunity to live out the Jewish value of *shalom bayit*—building home and family life on the tenets of mutual respect, love, and peacefulness—and to model a healthy relationship for your child. Greet your spouse when he or she returns home—drop everything (unless you are changing a diaper!)—and let your child see your excitement at being together again. Speak kindly and lovingly of one another, and let your child see you hug, kiss, and behave affectionately. This is truly one of the best things you can do— for your marriage and for your little one. Our children feel so happy, so secure, and so confident when they live in a home rooted in the principles of *shalom bayit*. And it will be good for you and your partner as well.

Of course, there will be times we will fight with our partners—we may differ on how to discipline our children, or feel stressed about issues at work or home, or even be nursing a real and legitimate grievance. We may feel resentful, unappreciated, bitter, or angry. These emotions are hard to contain, particularly if we lack a support system or have a hard time confessing our troubles to friends. At such times we may feel tempted to bring our children into the situation: slighting our spouses in front of them, or winning them over with extra treats or privileges, or even sharing our complaints. Please, don't do any of these things. They will damage your marriage, and they will damage your children. While conflicts inevitably arise, children should not witness or overhear their being played out.

Our children need our unconditional love and care—and they also need our firm and consistent guidance. Through positive reinforcement, logical consequences, and our own confidence in "being the boss," we can provide our children with these essential gifts. This system of discipline will help us do so. This system of discipline will teach our children before

---

[8]Proverbs 29:17–18, excerpted.

whom they stand—will teach them to respect us, to respect our rules, to respect what we do and say. This system of discipline will help us cope with, and correct, our children's misbehavior, without ever losing sight of our boundless love. And this system of discipline will, finally, enable our children to accept the consequences of their actions, and to make good choices.

A Still, Small Voice: Giving Instruction and Responding to Misbehavior

In Chapter 2, I alluded to the power of God's still, small voice. Its power—and its beauty—can be ours as well.

In the Book of First Kings, we find the prophet Elijah on the run. The faithless Queen Jezebel wants him dead, and he has spent forty days and forty nights fleeing through the wilderness, finally reaching shelter in a cave at Mount Horeb. God calls to him there, and Elijah emerges, ready to behold the Presence of the Eternal. Here's what happens next:

"The Eternal passed by. There was a great and mighty wind, splitting rocks and shattering mountains...but the Eternal was not in the wind. After the wind, an earthquake—but the Eternal was not in the earthquake. After the earthquake, fire—but the Eternal was not in the fire. And after the fire—a still, small voice."[9] It is here that Elijah encounters God. God is made known to Elijah not in drama and tumult, not in noise and din—but in quietude and in serenity. God understands the strength of the still, small voice.

We understand its strength as well. The still, small voice is our key to successful communication with our little ones—and their key to respectful communication with us.

Let me be clear: A still, small voice is not a voice of weakness or vulnerability. Rather, a still, small voice is calm, composed, confident enough in its power that it need not employ screaming or dramatics. If you don't

---

[9]1 Kings 19:11–12. The previous paragraph summarizes 1 Kings 19:2–11.

yet feel possessed of a still, small voice, that's totally understandable. It's not something we're born with, and it doesn't always come naturally. But with practice, and belief in yourself, it *will* come. Remember: You are your children's parent. You are important. You are doing sacred work. You deserve to be heard, and heeded.

Keep this in mind when you are telling your child what to do—especially if, like so many parents, you find yourself dreading this task. Sometimes even the most assertive, self-possessed among us seem to fall apart when it's time to issue instructions to our little ones. We fear sparking tantrums, upsetting our children, making them angry at us, squelching their spirit—any number of things. So rather than asserting our authority and simply saying, "We've had a great time, and we'll be leaving in five minutes"—and sticking to it—or "I know you want that candy bar, but we aren't going to buy it," we find ourselves saying things like, "It's almost time to go, okay?" or "We can't buy that candy bar, okay?"—as if we are asking our little ones for permission. Or we couch our directives in elaborate justifications: "You need to sit nicely in your chair while you eat because if you keep jumping up and down, I'm afraid you'll choke. And if you keep running around with your food, you might spill something, and that will make a mess." While it's important to help our little ones understand the reasons behind the rules, we need not apologize for making and enforcing these rules—and we need not offer an explanation every time we tell our children to do something. Don't be afraid simply to use a still, small voice—a voice of loving but firm authority: "Please say goodbye to Yumi and come out to the car," "Please put that candy bar back on the shelf," "Please sit nicely in your chair." We are entitled to use this still, small voice, and to have our children respond. It worked for God, and it should work for us.

It will work even when our children are behaving challengingly, defiantly. One of the reasons our children misbehave, after all, is to test us. What will we do if they deliberately dump out a box of bristle blocks we have just finished cleaning up? How will we counter if they refuse to put on their shoes? Our children are looking for a reaction—the more dramatic, the better. And we can make bad behavior a lot less appealing simply by responding in a still, small voice—that is, matter-of-factly, resolutely, without undue emotion: "I see you dumped out the blocks we just cleaned up. If you can put them away yourself, you can keep all of your toys in your room. If you choose not to put the blocks away, I will put three of your toys in time-out for the day." "I see you don't want to put on your shoes. If you cooperate while I help you put them on, you can choose the CD we listen to in the car. If you don't cooperate, we won't be able to listen to your music." Then we calmly follow through, offering brief praise if they clean up or cooperate and matter-of-factly enforcing the consequence if they don't. When our little ones see that they can't generate much of a response from these antics, they'll look for other (hopefully more positive) ways to capture our attention.

Now, a still, small voice will not work every time. But even when our children fail to respond at first, we can nevertheless adhere to the principle of the still, small voice. Except in very specific circumstances (more on these below and in the next section), we should never yell at our children. I know this might sound like a virtually impossible standard, but please bear with me. Generally, I believe, we yell because we have lost control, because we don't know what else to do. So instead of yelling, sometimes we just need to take a moment to remember who is in control, and what we need to do.

When a verbal instruction or reprimand doesn't produce the desired effect, we often try again: we say pretty much the same thing, and it usually has pretty much the same effect—that is, none. The temptation then arises to say pretty much the same thing again, but in a louder, angrier voice, which may work—at least in the short term—but which actually teaches our children that they don't have to do what we say until we say it loudly and angrily. At some point, we'll lose our patience and yell at our children, whether from habit or from frustration that the loud and angry voice has stopped working its magic and we're now at a total loss.

In a definition credited to Albert Einstein, insanity is "doing the same thing over and over again and expecting different results." While parenting does lead to its own form of insanity, this is a manifestation we do well to avoid! If you've used your still, small voice to direct your child, and you're positive she heard you but she isn't obeying, don't do the same thing over and over again—that is, don't repeat yourself or start bargaining or cajoling. If you've told your little one it's time to leave the playground, and she doesn't come running, simply walk over, pick her up, and carry her to the stroller or the car. If your child is playing with a huge stick (my son always finds the biggest one with the most ready-to-poke-out-someone's-eye point) and doesn't put it down when you tell her to, walk over and take it away. If you've told your child to share a toy with her playmate and she ignores you, take the toy and hand it to the other child. This seems so obvious, but we have all seen so many parents either hollering the same instructions to impassive children, or entering into protracted negotiations before their little ones will deign to obey. When we speak to our children in a still, small voice—sparingly and evenly—but back up our words with action, they will learn that we mean what we say, and we will enjoy the luxury of saying it calmly, and only once.

If our children are accustomed to hearing us speak in a still, small voice, they will also respond more quickly when we do employ a loud or urgent tone. For issues of safety or of immediate importance, we should absolutely bypass our still, small voice and bring out the big guns. If your child darts into the street, or slips away from you in a public place, or you see a large dog running loose, or experience any type of what I call a "God-forbid scenario," follow your instincts and yell away. Because this is such a radically different method of communicating with your little one, he will know right away that you are serious and he will be quicker to do what you say.

As useful as the still, small voice is for us, it is equally essential for our children. They, however, may not be as keen on its importance—that is, on speaking in a quiet, respectful tone. Too often we permit our children to address us in ways that we would never tolerate from a spouse, friend, or even employer. Our children call, "I need milk!" and we run to get it. Our children scream, "I wanted the blue playdough!" and we apologize for handing them the wrong color. Our children demand, "Read it to me again," and we turn back to the first page. But they, too, will benefit from the lesson of the still, small voice.

We want our children to understand before whom they stand—and before whom they speak. How our little ones talk to us reflects—and influences—how they regard us, and how they treat us. By instilling respectful language in our children, we help instill respectful behavior.

This process can begin as soon as our little ones begin to speak. When encouraging your little one to use her words, teach her to say "more, please," "higher, please," or "again, please" rather than simply "more," "higher," or "again." When you ask your child if she wants something, prompt her to answer politely: "Which yogurt would you like—strawberry please or blueberry please?" or "Do you want help climbing into your carseat, yes please or no thank you?" Wait for your child to pronounce the entire phrase in a reasonably clear voice before honoring her request. (If she balks at adding the "please" or "thank you," don't turn the issue into a power struggle; just matter-of-factly tell her that you are ready to help her as soon as she speaks to you properly, then turn your attention to something else.) Before long these responses will become automatic for your little one—and although she might not yet understand the meaning of the words themselves, she will understand that she must speak to you in a certain way in order to get what she wants.

As our little ones grow, we can make more explicit their obligation to speak to us respectfully. If your three-year-old yells, "I want some pretzels!" or even the almost-acceptable, "I need help with my socks!" don't come running. Call back to him, "I'll be happy to listen to you as soon as you ask nicely," and wait till he does. After all, a child who is old enough to say "Bring me a spoon" is old enough to say "May I have a spoon please?"—and old enough to understand that he should.

Of course, our little ones will sometimes refuse to follow this rule—out of anger or frustration or stubbornness, perhaps, or simply to see what we will do in response. Rather than rephrase their requests in a respectful way, they may resort to rephrasing their requests in a louder, angrier way—or rephrasing it over-and-over-and-over-as-they-follow-us-around-the-house in a whiny way—or even casting the request aside entirely and saying rude or hurtful things. Because you cannot physically force your child to say words she has no intention of saying, don't try to threaten or cajole her into respectful speech. Instead, offer a controlled choice: "I hear that you don't want to speak respectfully, but I don't want to hear your angry (or whining) voice. If you choose to talk that way, you may talk that way in your room with the door closed. When you are ready to speak respectfully, come out and we can play together." Depending on how wrought up your little one is, you may need to lead her by the hand or even carry her to her room; do so firmly but as calmly and gently as possible. This is not intended as a punishment but as a logical consequence of how she has chosen to speak to you. And it will work to her benefit as well as yours: Sometimes the specter of time alone in her room will be all she needs to improve her behavior; sometimes what she really needs will be a stretch of time alone to cool off and get herself together. Either way, you avoid a power struggle—and both of you win.

This controlled choice will also work when your little one has approached you with a beautifully delivered, perfectly respectful appeal to watch a DVD or use the computer—then dissolved into angry howls or tearful whimpering when you thank him for his good manners but explain that he has already had enough screen time for the day. Let him scream or whine for a moment, then calmly say: "I hear you're upset, and it's okay to be upset, but the place for screaming (or whining) is in your room with the door closed. As soon as you're done screaming (or whining), come out and we'll play together." Once he calms down, do not allow him to belabor the request: "I've already told you no, and I'm all done talking about it. If you want to talk about it some more, you can talk about it to yourself in your room with the door closed." If this leads to more screaming or whining, simply repeat step one.

Again, you are not punishing your child for being upset; she has the right to yell and fuss and complain just as we do—and just as we do, she's going to exercise that right now and then. You are, however, teaching her the important lesson that she cannot subject everyone around her to her yelling and fussing and complaining. While her feelings are important and worthy of expression, they do not override the feelings of those around her. Her right to express anger, disappointment, and frustration does not trump our right to a reasonably quiet, serene, respectful atmosphere.[10]

✿

God was not in the wind, or the earthquake, or the fire. True communication, true sharing with our children, cannot flourish amid screaming and shouting, amid tumult and turmoil. It was only in the quietude, the serenity, the gentleness that Elijah could hear the voice of God. And it is in the still, small voice that we—and our little ones—can hear, and truly listen to, one another.

Ouch! Throwing Toys, Hitting, and Biting

It's okay for our children to get angry. They should never feel forced to hide their bad moods, never fear sharing their disappointment, frustration, even rage. It's our job to make sure our children can communicate these complex and difficult emotions.

However, sometimes our children's feelings ignite wounding behavior. Sometimes our children react by lashing out at those around them. Sometimes our children throw toys, hit, or bite when they are sad or angry. And that is absolutely *not* okay.

We must walk a fine line, respecting our little ones' darker emotions while still managing their behavior. But as important as it is for our children to express themselves, it is just as important for them to recognize the limits of that expression. In words made famous by Oliver Wendell Holmes: "The right to swing my fist ends where the other [person]'s nose begins." Our children's right to express themselves ends when they hurt other people.

---

[10]Of course, I am speaking about the everyday indignities of being a toddler or preschooler: thwarted desires for sweets, toys, privileges, and the like, or resentment of consequences for misbehavior. When our children are sick, hurt, or dealing with serious issues, they need us by their side and actively involved in helping them express their feelings.

When our little ones physically hurt someone else, our first responsibility is to do what it takes to stop that behavior. If your child deliberately throws a toy at, hits, or bites another child, you must step in immediately. This is no time for the still, small voice; rather, pick up your child, look directly at him, and say loudly, "No! We do not throw toys! (Or we do not hit! We do not bite!)" Take him away from the group and tell him firmly, "It's okay to be angry, but it is not okay to throw toys (or hit or bite). If you're angry, you can say 'I'm angry' or you can bang on a pillow (or couch or rug), but you may not throw toys (or hit or bite)." If he is flailing around, hold him in your lap with his back to you, your arms restraining his arms and legs until he calms down, saying: "I know you want to hit, but you may not hit. I will hold your arms to stop you from hitting until you can stop yourself." When he has settled down (this may take awhile, but it will happen) you can decide whether to return to the group for apologies to the hurt child and try again, or whether it's best just to leave. If you do return and he repeats the same behavior, however, there can be no third chance.

This is an intense response, but an important one. When we dismiss our children's aggressive behavior with a "Honey, that's not nice," or "She's just really tired," or "You're really upset, aren't you, baby? Come here and I'll snuggle you," we are doing a tremendous disservice to them—and to their playmates. Only by reacting strongly when our little ones hurt another can we demonstrate that their behavior is unacceptable—and ensure that it won't become a regular thing. We must help our children cope with their emotions in a healthy and controlled way (more on this below), not excuse their outbursts in the name of self-expression.

It may be easier to employ these consequences when we are looking right at the injured victim—and seething caregiver. But what if our little ones lash out at us? What if our children deliberately throw toys at, hit, or bite us?

We have all seen it, and perhaps even lived it: a child really waling on his parent, the parent tolerating the beating, emitting only an occasional —and ineffectual—"Sweetie, that hurts," or "I know you're angry," or even "please stop." It is painful to see—no doubt even more painful to experience—and it is absolutely wrong.

The medieval Rabbi Ahai taught: "The rule that '[parents] may forgo the honor due [them]' applies to [their] honor. But [they] must not allow [themselves] to be struck."[11] Ideally, all parents will insist that their children treat them with honor. This is how our children learn their place in the world, and learn to conduct themselves properly. Unfortunately, some parents do not instill this lesson in their little ones. As Rabbi Ahai observes, some parents forgo the honor due them—some parents permit their children to treat them disrespectfully. This is the wrong choice, but it is the parents' choice to make.

Some behavior, however, cannot be excused, or accepted. Parents "must not allow [themselves] to be struck." No matter how reluctant we might be to invoke our authority, to discipline our children, to say "no," we *must* stop our children from hurting us physically. I think Rabbi Ahai's ruling stems from an essential truth: Letting our children hurt us is one of the worst things we can do to them. As parents, we are supposed to be our children's rocks, anchors, protectors. How can our little ones possibly trust us to keep them safe when they can so easily overwhelm us? How can our children possibly trust us to defend them against any kind of imagined danger when we can't even defend ourselves against them? If your child deliberately throws a toy at you, hits you, or bites you, you must stop her immediately. If you are hesitant to do so for your own sake, then do it for hers.

How can we stop this behavior? We can do it by making the consequence so unpleasant that our children will not want to experience it again. While you must never lose control of yourself (and must never, of course, hit or bite your child back), your reaction should strongly affect your little one. Different techniques will work for different families. You can get down on your child's level, look him directly in the eye, and in a very loud and dramatic voice say: "No! You do not hit (or bite) me! You never hit (or bite) me!" If you and your little one are in a childproofed room, turn around, walk out, close the door firmly, and leave your child alone for a moment. Otherwise, turn him around so his back is to you and either put him by himself in a safe room or hold him firmly and tell

---

[11]In Telushkin, *Jewish Wisdom*, 154.

him: "You may not hurt me. I will hold you to stop you from hurting me until you can stop yourself." Your response should upset your little one, which is actually a good thing; he will come to associate his actions with your reaction, and find another way to express his anger in the future. Ideally—and very likely if you respond appropriately—he will not hit or bite you again.

Although our primary responsibility is to stop our little ones from hurting others, we should also teach them appropriate ways to express and manage their more difficult emotions. Again, our goal is never to have our little ones repress or deny their darker feelings; that would ultimately prove just as destructive as hitting or biting. When you see your little one getting frustrated, gently intervene: "It's tough when the block tower keeps falling down, isn't it? Let's get a snack and try again a little later," or "I see you're feeling upset. Take a deep breath with me; then we'll count to five and let it out. Good! Let's try that again." Model healthy anger management: "I got so mad at work today! It was hard not to yell at my boss. But I took a walk, and then I felt better," or "I'm angry that you drew on the walls. I'm going to go in the other room to calm down, and then we'll talk about your consequence." Take time to discuss emotions and how to handle them; when your little one is well-rested and in a good mood, have her role-play sad or angry feelings and suggest ways she might resolve them—from using her words to smacking a pillow to drawing a picture. My daughter's Mommy and Me instructors do an amazing job of this; they adapted the words of "If You're Happy and You Know It" to familiarize their students with experiencing and expressing anger. ("If you're angry and you know it, stomp your feet," "If you're angry and you know it, blow it out," and "If you're angry and you know it, say 'I'm mad'"—brilliant!) If these tactics do not dissuade your child's outbursts, or if you feel genuinely frightened by her behavior, talk to your pediatrician.

The Book of Proverbs teaches: "A furious person abounds in transgression."[12] When we are furious, we are prone to transgression—we are likely to do the wrong thing. We demonstrate our strength of

---

[12]Proverbs 29:22.

character by controlling our anger, by channeling and finally conquering it. It's not easy for us, and it won't be easy for our children, either. But it will be easier for them if they begin to learn early, and if we help. And, as the Book of Proverbs continues, mastering these emotions is the key to living with honor.[13]

I'm Not Tired! Sleeping, Revisited

Bathing our little ones and bundling them in warm pajamas, snuggling in the rocker and enjoying a story, singing the *Sh'ma* and tucking the blanket around our children's sweet bodies can make bedtime one of the most delicious parts of the day. Whether we keep our little ones in bed with us or put them to sleep in cribs, big-kid beds, or even pop-up tents (my friend's son slept in one for years and loved it; he called it his nest), we all savor the feel and the sight of a blissfully sleeping child.

For some of us, however, this blissfully sleeping child proves a bit elusive during the toddler and preschool years. It is a time of such intense challenge and change for our children, and even the most cooperative sleeper—not to mention the rest of our little ones—may reflect the upheaval in his nighttime and naptime behavior. He may demonstrate his longing for freedom and independence by sauntering out of his room moments after you've put him to bed or refusing to nap even when it's painfully obvious he's exhausted; he may demonstrate his fear of that same freedom and independence by resisting sleeping on his own or crying about monsters in the closet. As always, our job as parents is to respect our children's needs for self-expression and support while still guiding them toward appropriate behavior.

This may not be easy. After a long day, we may have a difficult time summoning the energy and patience to instill proper bedtime behavior. If we've been home with our little ones, we may be exhausted from the demands of parenting; if we've been working outside the house, we may

---

[13]Proverbs 29:23.

be tempted to go against our better judgment in order to make our time with our children as enjoyable as possible. In either case, it's much easier (in the short term at least) to indulge our children's demands that we lie down with them until they doze off, or tolerate their climbing into our beds at 3 A.M., or bring them a midnight bottle or sippy cup if they "promise to go right back to sleep" if we do. But these practices are not good for our children in the long term; our children need to be taught good sleep skills, and no one except us appears to be lining up for the job.

I think our primary goals are to teach our little ones that they are safe in their beds, and that that is where they belong. Teaching our little ones that they are safe in their beds speaks to their needs for reassurance and nurturing. Teaching our little ones that they belong in their beds speaks to their needs for learning their place and respecting our authority.

We cannot take for granted that our children feel safe in their beds (or cribs—I will use the terms interchangeably here). The beautifully decorated nursery, the hand-painted walls, the painstakingly selected quilt and dust ruffle may represent love and security to us but aloneness and vulnerability to our little ones. Particularly during these years—when our little ones are clinging to us one moment and pushing us away the next, modeling themselves after us yet defying us—confronting the night on their own can be very intimidating and very scary. In order to teach our children to sleep well in their beds, then, we must first help them understand that bed is a safe and wonderful place.

How can we do this? Although we adults are advised to help prevent insomnia by using our beds almost exclusively for sleep, our little ones can develop positive feelings about going to bed by hanging out there during the day. If you're reading or doing a puzzle or making a sticker picture with your little one, set up the activity on her bed. Let her jump on the bed—at least once in a while—or turn off the lights, snuggle under the sheets, and wave flashlights around to create shooting stars. Make her bed as inviting and welcoming as possible; even if it interferes with the room's décor, encourage her to display some of her favorite toys—even blocks or trucks—on the bed, and to tuck in her dolls and stuffed animals. Finally, talk to your child in a straightforward and supportive manner: "I know you don't like going to bed by yourself, or staying in your own bed at night, and I know that it is scary for you. I hope that playing on your bed and keeping your trucks on your bed will help you remember that you are safe in your bed. Bed is a safe place."

As nighttime looms, we can underscore these words with a soothing and supportive bedtime ritual. Although your reading, singing, and offering a prayer may still play an important role in the routine, most toddlers and preschoolers are ready to take a more active part. After dimming the lights, invite your child to sit on your lap and talk about the best and worst parts of his day, what he wants to do tomorrow, or whatever is on his mind. He can take a moment to share these thoughts with God as well—either speaking aloud or silently. One of my friends created another meaningful bedtime custom; every night, her daughter tells what she is most thankful for, and my friend writes down the responses in a notebook titled "Grateful Journal."

If your little one suffers from nighttime fears—of monsters, for example—make your reassurances a part of her bedtime ritual. Rather than humoring her by proffering a bottle of "monster spray" or checking under the bed and in the closet one-more-time (these tactics suggest that you, too, believe these monsters are real, and can be kept at bay only through magic and watchfulness), try to deal with what her fears might represent. Some children, afraid of their own aggressive or hurtful impulses, personify them as monsters; other children envision as monsters the stressors in their daily lives. (And some really are scared of three-headed beasts that allegedly lurk in darkened rooms!) Ask your little one what she imagines these monsters will look like, or what they will do; you will probably gain some insight into the root of her fears, plus your hearing her out will make her more amenable to listening to you. When she finishes speaking, empathize that these monsters really do sound scary, then tell her: "Sometimes when we get angry, or want to hurt other people, we start to think about monsters. Sometimes when we feel worried or upset, we start to think about monsters. But I promise monsters are not real. It's okay to be angry, and it's okay to be worried. But even when we are worried or upset, monsters are not real.

Even when you are worried or upset, I will keep you safe." Your little one may find further comfort in a paraphrase of the traditional nighttime *Hashkiveinu* prayer: "Help us, O God, to lie down in peace, and to wake up again in peace. Shield us and protect us, and watch over our comings and our goings, now and forever."

Just before you turn out the light and leave the room, gently remind your little one of the bedtime rules and what you expect from him during the night. Be clear and specific, acknowledging his feelings but setting firm guidelines: "Tonight you must go to sleep in your bed and stay in your bed all night. I know you like to come sleep in my bed, but that is not a choice. You are safe in your bed, and that is where you belong. If you feel sad during the night, hug your bear (if he isn't attached to any particular stuffed animal, you could give him one of your old shirts to sleep with instead) and remember that I love you."

Use this basic *shpiel* for any nighttime behavior you are working on, keeping things as positive as possible—but also being ready to stand firm if (or when) your little one resists. Of course you can promise to check on her frequently (be sure to follow through, but not so much that you distract her from actually falling asleep) and offer rewards for staying in her own bed; but lying down with your little one until she falls asleep when you've already said you wouldn't, or letting her come out for endless hugs and kisses and drinks of water when you've already instructed her to stay in her room, or permitting her to crawl into your bed when you've already told her to sleep in her own, undercuts not only your parental authority but also your promise that bed is safe. After all, if she is really so safe in bed, and that's really where she is supposed to be, why are her parents acting so uncertain?

Before reciting the *Sh'ma* at bedtime, Jews traditionally offer this prayer to God: "You are blessed, Eternal One our God, Sovereign of the world, Who closes our eyes in sleep, our eyelids in slumber. May You let me sleep in peace, and awaken in peace. May my rest be perfect before You." It's scary to close our eyes for the night, to hand over control to our subconscious—and to God. Bedtime prayers demonstrate that it is not only children who feel especially vulnerable when it's time to sleep.

But just as we've learned to trust in God and our miraculous bodies, so can we instill this trust in our little ones. Just as we know we're safe and healthy in our beds, so can we bring this knowledge to our children. And just as we've grown to savor the blessing of rest, so can we teach the joy of sleep.

May our rest be peaceful and abundant—and always perfect before God.

Made in the Image of God: Not (Overly) Complaining About Your Little One

As we know so well, each of us is different; this is, the Talmud teaches, a testament to the greatness of God. "[I]f a person strikes many coins from one die, they all resemble one another; in fact, they are all exactly alike. But though the Sovereign of sovereigns, the Holy One, blessed be God, fashioned every human being from the die of the first human being, not a single one is exactly like another."[14] Sometimes we struggle with these differences; other times we embrace them as what make us singular and special—as reminders that we are created in the image of God.

And just as each of us is different, so is each of our children different. Sometimes we struggle with these differences, too—why is my little one still crying for his paci when the other kids in playgroup happily gave theirs up to the paci fairy? Why does my child pee but refuse to poop on the potty when the other kids in his class are totally toilet trained? Why does my little one sit on the sidelines at birthday parties instead of joining the fun with the other kids? Is there something wrong with my child? Is there something wrong with me?

Although some differences may require attention and intervention (always check with your pediatrician for an objective and expert opinion), many are just part of being created singular and special. And while these differences can be frustrating, they can also help us see and appreciate our

---

[14]*Sanhedrin* 38a, in Bialik 14:54.

children's uniqueness—and remind us that they are created in the image of God.

We can change so much just by changing our attitude. Instead of thinking, "My child doesn't know all her letters," try "My child is learning her letters." Instead of thinking, "My child isn't participating in the group," try, "My child likes to observe." Instead of thinking, "My child is driving me nuts," try, "My child is determined and energetic." As simplistic as this may sound, it really works. Our children are more attuned than we realize to what we think about them; if our little ones grow accustomed to being regarded as slow, or unsociable, or annoying, that is how they will come to see themselves, and how they will behave. When we focus on the positive, we offer our children the chance to grow, to flourish, to succeed—and offer ourselves the chance to feel more patient, more hopeful, more upbeat.

As much as our outlook affects our little ones, our words affect them still more. A Jewish legend illustrates the power of words: A woman came to her rabbi seeking counsel. For years, she confessed, she had spoken cruelly of others, spreading insults, gossip, and half-truths. She felt terrible for all she'd done and desperately wanted to make amends. The rabbi listened carefully, then told her to take a feather pillow, climb a high hill, tear open the case, and let the feathers fall free. The woman did as instructed, then returned to the rabbi. "Now," the rabbi said, "go and collect all the feathers."

The words we speak to—and about—our children are like those feathers. We may release them without realizing their symbolic power, and we cannot take them back. When in the heat of anger we tell our little ones, "You never listen to me!" or "When are you going to stop using that stupid binky?" or "Stop acting like such a brat!" we may not realize how hurtful and damaging our words are—but once we do, we cannot take them back. When we complain to friends that our children are "whining again" or "the last one his age in diapers" or "a terrible eater," we may not realize how our words are betraying our children's trust in us as their champions and defenders—but once we do, we cannot take them back.

Our challenges are real, and our aggravations are legitimate. Pretending our little ones are perfect, that our lives are always unfolding smoothly and blissfully, is exhausting—for us, for our children, and for those forced to listen to us prattling on. We need a safe space, and close friends we can trust, to express our darkest thoughts about parenthood. But there is a time and a place for these conversations, and it is not when we are in the presence of casual acquaintances, or surrounded by strangers, or within earshot of our children. When we speak of our little ones—especially when they are listening, but even when they are not—we must remember that we are speaking of those created in the image of God.

7

Conclusion

Nearly two thousand years ago our Sages contemplated God's creation. They apprehended the world's amazing beauty, but they also saw its terrible flaws; and they dared to believe that God shared their disappointment in these shortcomings. Playing with the words of the Creation story, they imagined God viewing the divine handiwork and saying not "Behold, it was very good"—but rather "Would that it were always very good."[1] Continued Rav Hama bar Hanina: "The Holy One said to [the] world: 'My world, My world! May you find favor in My eyes at all times just as you find favor in My eyes at this moment.'"[2]

When God's world was newly born, it was very good. It found favor in God's eyes. But as our ancient Sages taught—and as we know only too well—much has happened since the days of Creation. The world today is not always worthy of God's favor. The world today is not always worthy of our children.

And yet it is our precious children who carry the promise of our world perfected. According to Jewish folk wisdom, with every child the world

---

[1]Genesis 1:31.
[2]Genesis *Rabbah* 9:4, in Bialik 19:72.

begins anew. With each child comes love, and innocence, and radiance, and beauty. With each child comes a pure soul, a unique spirit. With each child comes the possibility of peace. With each child comes the hope of redemption.

We say with God, "Would that it were always very good." Would that our little ones continue to bring life and light and goodness to God's Creation, and would that we who share our children's world make it deserving of them. And may our little ones—and we who love them—find favor always in God's eyes, as surely they find favor in God's eyes at this moment.

APPENDIX A

The Radiance in Our Faces
Blessings and Rituals for Shabbat

In the Book of Genesis we read that after creating the world in six days, "God blessed the seventh day, and sanctified it."[1] Jewish tradition adds that God blessed Shabbat with the radiance of human faces. The radiance of our faces during the week is not the same as the radiance of our faces on Shabbat.[2]

Our ancient Sages were onto something. As radiant as our precious children are—and as radiant as they inspire us to be—there is a still more special radiance that comes with Shabbat. Shabbat is glorious: a day set aside for rest and refreshment, for family and friends, for thanksgiving and for taking stock of what is truly essential. Shabbat is a day for God, and it is a gift for us. All we need is to accept it.

But how? Restricting our use of electricity, driving, and writing may feel more archaic than meaningful. Preparing an elaborate meal may feel

---

[1] Genesis 2:3.
[2] *B'reishit Rabbah* 11:2.

more stressful than festive. And mastering the traditional prayers and practices may feel more daunting than celebratory.

Yet God has given us so many ways to bring the radiance of Shabbat into our home and into our family life. We can start small. Perhaps we will be inspired to deeper and fuller Shabbat observance, which is wonderful. Or perhaps we will stay small, which is also wonderful. But we owe it to ourselves and to our children to make Shabbat holy. We owe it to God to let God make our faces radiant with the divine gift of Shabbat.

We can begin, as Shabbat does, with Friday night. Although Tot Shabbat or family services at synagogue can be a treat, Friday night observance is traditionally centered in the home. This doesn't mean we need five-course meals and starched white tablecloths and freshly ironed clothes (though if this sounds appealing, go for it!). What it does mean is that our Friday nights should not be like every other night. Friday nights should be special.

What will we need? The ceremonial objects for Friday nights are a pair of candlesticks, a *Kiddush* cup, and a challah cover. Some families add an extra candlestick for each child, or have a *tzedakah* box as well. While any candlesticks, a plain wineglass, and a napkin will suffice, having special pieces set aside for Shabbat will infuse the rituals with extra significance. If you have heirloom items, take them out of the china cabinet and put them to use. Otherwise, you can find beautiful pieces at Judaica and synagogue gift shops, or you and your child can fashion your own. Cover a box, can, or paper towel roll with construction paper or stickers, then cut a hole in the top to collect *tzedakah*; use clay or empty baby-food jars decorated with glitter glue to hold candles; make a tissue-paper collage on a plastic wineglass to craft a *Kiddush* cup; and sew or glue buttons and beads to a piece of felt to cover challah. Speaking of challah, if you are feeling especially ambitious, you can invite your child to create a challah plate from one of those make-a-plate kits, or have him join you for baking homemade challah. (You'll find an unbelievably easy and delicious recipe at the end of this appendix.)

As Shabbat approaches, remind your little one of the Shabbat objects' significance and let her help you set them out: "Why don't you arrange the shiny candlesticks my grandma gave us, and I'll take the beautiful *Kiddush* cup and challah cover you made for our family?" Consider changing clothes before beginning the Shabbat meal; the new outfits need not be formal or fancy, just something you enjoy wearing and feel good in—from (in my sons' case) a reasonably clean shirt to (in my daughter's case) a Snow White or Cinderella gown with matching shoes.

Once your family is ready to sit down, tell your little one in an upbeat voice how happy you are that the week is over and that it is time to celebrate Shabbat. You might begin the meal by singing *z'mirot*, special songs for Shabbat; you can choose tunes composed especially for children, or introduce your little one to traditional, easy-to-sing favorites like "*Bim Bam*" and "*Shalom Alecheim*." (There are literally hundreds of *z'mirot* out there; ask your rabbi or cantor for suggestions, or look online or at Judaica or synagogue gift shops.) When you are ready to begin the blessings, explain to your little one that Shabbat is a happy time but also a holy time, and that you expect him to listen quietly to (or participate in, as he gets older) the prayers. Involve him as much as possible: Give him some coins to drop in the *tzedakah* box; turn off the lights before kindling the candles so he (and you) can better appreciate their warm glow; let him help hold the *Kiddush* cup (or give him his own); and ask him to pull off the challah cover when it's time for *HaMotzi*. You can even give him his own special blessing; bestowing the traditional Shabbat blessings upon our children is one of the greatest and most joyous privileges of Jewish parenthood. All of these blessings can be found at the end of this appendix.

Now, of course, it's time to eat! Shabbat dinner should be special—but if your family's Shabbat meal doesn't resemble the traditional chicken-and-sweet-kugel fare, don't give it a second thought. Your family's idea of a special meal might be Thai take-out, or drive-through fried chicken, or macaroni and cheese, or chocolate milk, or an extra scoop of ice cream for dessert. It really doesn't matter; do what works for your family, not what-you-think-you-are-supposed-to-do-even-though-it-will-exhaust-you-and-make-you-miserable-and-keep-you-from-actually-enjoying-Shabbat.

Although it's tough with a toddler (easier with a preschooler, but still not easy!), try to make dinnertime conversation special as well. Share with your child a story or lesson from the weekly Torah portion, or chat about a Jewish value or upcoming Jewish holiday. Ask questions as basic as "What letter do you think 'God' starts with?" or "What's your favorite Shabbat blessing?" or as challenging as "I bet Moses was really scared to tell Pharaoh to let the Jewish people go. What do you think you would have done?" or "Why do you think the Torah says it's wrong to steal?" You can find wonderful resources online for these discussions, or consult with your rabbi, cantor, or Jewish educator for ideas. If your child is too young, or just not ready for this level of talk, you might want to read her a brief book about Shabbat instead, so she comes to associate the blessings and meal with the meaning of Shabbat. (Suggested titles are listed at the end of this appendix.)

As your family grows accustomed to celebrating Shabbat on Friday nights, you may come to continue your observance on Saturday. After all, Shabbat does last for a full day, and there are so many meaningful ways to spend it. Learn about the traditional Shabbat restrictions and practices; while they may not speak to you as-is, they may inspire you to refrain from—or embrace—certain activities in order to sanctify the day. While you may not leave the lights off all day, for example, perhaps your family will institute a no-morning-television-or-computer rule, in favor of reading, playing, or just snuggling together. While you may not stay out of your car all day, perhaps your family will take a long walk, or enjoy an hour or two outside. And while you may not be able to ignore work all day, perhaps you can do only what really, truly cannot wait, and devote some extra time to what—and who—matters most.

Because every family is different, no two Shabbat observances will look exactly the same. And that is fine, for there are many ways to make the day holy, and many ways to experience the unique radiance God brings to our faces—and the faces of our children—on Shabbat.

Blessings Over the Candles, Wine, and Challah

בָּרוּךְ אַתָּה יְיָ, אֱלֹהֵינוּ מֶלֶךְ הָעוֹלָם, אֲשֶׁר קִדְּשָׁנוּ בְּמִצְוֹתָיו
וְצִוָּנוּ לְהַדְלִיק נֵר שֶׁל שַׁבָּת.

Baruch atah Adonai Eloheinu Melech haolam, asher ḳidshanu b'mitzvotav vetzivanu l'hadliḳ ner shel Shabbat.

You are blessed, Eternal One our God, Sovereign of the world, Who makes us holy with Your commandments and commands us to kindle the lights of Shabbat.

בָּרוּךְ אַתָּה יְיָ, אֱלֹהֵינוּ מֶלֶךְ הָעוֹלָם, בּוֹרֵא פְּרִי הַגָּפֶן.

Baruch atah Adonai Eloheinu Melech haolam, borei p'ri hagafen.

You are blessed, Eternal One our God, Sovereign of the world, Who creates the fruit of the vine.

בָּרוּךְ אַתָּה יְיָ, אֱלֹהֵינוּ מֶלֶךְ הָעוֹלָם, הַמּוֹצִיא לֶחֶם מִן הָאָרֶץ.

Baruch atah Adonai Eloheinu Melech haolam, hamotzi lechem min ha'aretz.

You are blessed, Eternal One our God, Sovereign of the world, Who brings forth bread from the earth.

Blessings for Our Children

Place your hands on your child's head, look into his or her eyes, and say:

FOR BOYS:

יְשִׂימְךָ אֱלֹהִים כְּאֶפְרַיִם וְכִמְנַשֶּׁה.

Y'simcha Elohim ḳ'Efrayim v'chiMenasheh.

May God inspire you to live like Ephraim and Manasseh.

FOR GIRLS:

יְשִׂימֵךְ אֱלֹהִים כְּשָׂרָה, כְּרִבְקָה כְּרָחֵל וּכְלֵאָה.

Y'simeich Elohim ḳ'Sarah, ḳ'Rivḳah, ḳ'Rachel, uchLeah.

May God inspire you to live like Sarah, Rebecca, Rachel, and Leah.

FOR BOTH, OFFER THE PRIESTLY BENEDICTION:

יְבָרֶכְךָ יְיָ וְיִשְׁמְרֶךָ.

יָאֵר יְיָ פָּנָיו אֵלֶיךָ וִיחֻנֶּךָ.

יִשָּׂא יְיָ פָּנָיו אֵלֶיךָ וְיָשֵׂם לְךָ שָׁלוֹם.

Y'varech'cha Adonai v'yishm'recha.

Ya-eir Adonai panav eilecha vichuneka.

Yisa Adonai panav eilecha v'yaseim l'cha shalom.

May God bless you and keep you.

May God shine upon you, and may God be gracious to you.

May you feel God's Presence within you always, and may you find peace.

A Great Challah Recipe

Little ones can help with virtually any step in this recipe. It is so easy and fun, and the challah is absolutely delicious! When it's time to braid the challah, consider making slightly smaller loaves and giving some dough to your child; my kids love forming it into "creative challahs" (letters, animals, and the like) or decorating it with chocolate chips. Yum!

You will need these ingredients:

2 cups of warm water
Scant 1 cup plus 1 tsp. sugar
6 ½ cups bread flour (have some extra bread flour on hand, too)
2 packets (or 5 tsp.) yeast
2 tsp. salt
1 egg
½ cup oil (have some extra oil on hand, too)

Mix 1 cup of warm water with 1 teaspoon sugar. Add yeast and stir gently. Set it aside as it bubbles; if it doesn't bubble within 15 minutes, the yeast is dead—try this part again with fresh yeast.

MEANWHILE…

In a separate bowl, mix the rest of the ingredients with 1 cup of warm water. Then add the yeast mixture. Knead it all together till it is well-mixed and only a little sticky; use a little extra flour and sugar if needed. Form the dough into a large ball. Lightly oil a large bowl, then put the dough inside, flipping the dough over till it too is lightly coated with oil. Cover and set aside for 1–2 hours.

THEN...

Lightly flour your hands and a workspace. Punch down the dough and divide it into 2 big pieces. Then take each big piece and divide it into 3 long strips for braiding (you will have 6 strips total that will make 2 braided challah loaves). Braid the loaves and place each one on a separate baking sheet that has been lightly sprayed with oil. Cover and set aside 1 hour.

THEN...

Preheat the oven to 350 degrees. Make an egg wash if desired; beat 1 egg with some water in a bowl (stir in a bit of honey for an extra treat!) then lightly brush it over the challah. Bake 20–35 minutes; the time depends on your oven and the thickness of your challah loaves, so check on the challah after 20 minutes so it won't overcook.

Enjoy!

Shabbat Books for Adults

A Day Apart: Shabbat at Home, by Noam Zion. Shalom Hartman Institute.

Gates of Shabbat: A Guide for Observing Shabbat, by Mark Dov Shapiro. CCAR Press.

An Invitation to Shabbat, by Ruth Perelson. URJ Press.

The Modern Jewish Mom's Guide to Shabbat: Connect and Celebrate—Bring your Family Together with the Friday Night Meal, by Meredith L. Jacobs. Harper Paperbacks.

The Sabbath, by Abraham Joshua Heschel. Farrar Straus Giroux.

Shabbat: The Family Guide to Preparing for and Welcoming the Sabbath, by Ron Wolfson. Jewish Lights Publishing.

A Shabbat Reader: Universe of Cosmic Joy, edited by Dov Peretz Elkins. URJ Press.

Shabbat Books for Children

Becky and Benny Thank God, written and illustrated by Howard I. Bogot. CCAR Press.

Mrs. Moskowitz and the Sabbath Candlesticks, written and illustrated by Amy Schwartz. Jewish Publication Society of America.

My First Shabbat Board Book, DK Publishing.

Sammy Spider's First Shabbat, by Sylvia A. Rouss, illustrated by Katherine Janus Kahn. Kar-Ben Publishing.

The Seventh Day, by Deborah Bodin Cohen, illustrated by Melanie W. Hall. Kar-Ben Publishing.

Shabbat Shalom! by Michelle Shapiro Abraham, illustrated by Ann D. Koffsky. URJ Press.

Shavua Tov! by Michelle Shapiro Abraham, illustrated by Ann D. Koffsky. URJ Press.

Soft Shapes: My Shabbat, Innovative Kids Publishing.

Tot Shabbat, written and illustrated by Camille Kress. URJ Press.

APPENDIX B

And You Shall Rejoice Before the Eternal Your God

Holiday Fun and Observance for Young Families

I t's easy to let the Jewish holidays slide past with little if any notice. After all, Sukkot doesn't get exactly the same buildup as Thanksgiving, and no one is sitting on a seder plate's lap at the mall listing the gifts they want for Passover. Most of our holidays don't appear on secular calendars, the dates (at least the Gregorian ones) change every year anyway, and our lives may feel busy and full enough without delving into the observance of seemingly minor festivals.

But like Shabbat, the Jewish holidays are God's precious gift to us. They help us mark time in a significant way, recall the sacred moments in our people's history, and impart the values we hold most dear. Oh, and most of them are a lot of fun, too! With a little effort, we can enable our children—and ourselves—to experience the holidays with meaning and with gladness, and to fulfill the divine command: "You shall celebrate the festival of the Eternal...and you shall rejoice before the Eternal your God."[1]

In the following pages you will find information and guidance to help you get started: a description of each holiday, an explanation of traditions associated with it, ideas for bringing the holiday alive for children, and a list of books your little one might enjoy. While the Hebrew dates for the festivals are the same every year, the Gregorian dates do change, so you will also need a Jewish calendar (available at Judaica and synagogue gift shops, or online at hebcal.com) to tell you on which days to celebrate. If you wish to learn more about these holidays, I recommend *Gates of the Seasons* and *To Be a Jew* (these books provide a liberal and Orthodox perspective, respectively)[2] as well as the Web sites for the Union of Reform Judaism (urj.org), the United Synagogue for Conservative Judaism (uscj.org), and the Orthodox Union (ou.org). Your rabbi, cantor, or Jewish educator will be an invaluable resource as well.

Get ready to rejoice!

The High Holy Days: Rosh Hashanah and Yom Kippur

Literally meaning "head of the year," Rosh Hashanah falls on the first day of the Hebrew month of Tishrei and heralds the start of the Jewish new year. Rosh Hashanah is also understood as the "birthday of the world" and the anniversary of the day God created human beings. Perhaps most significant, Rosh Hashanah begins the "Ten Days of Repentance," a time for taking stock of our lives and our good and bad deeds of the past year; these days culminate in Yom Kippur—the Jewish Day of Atonement. Yom Kippur is the holiest and most solemn occasion on the Jewish calendar, a day of reflection and seeking pardon from those—including and especially God—whom we have wronged.

---

[1]Leviticus 23:39, 40.
[2]*Gates of the Seasons: A Guide to the Jewish Year* is edited by Rabbi Peter Knobel and published by CCAR Press; *To Be a Jew* is written by Rabbi Hayim Halevy Donin and published by Basic Books, a division of HarperCollins Publishers.

TRADITIONAL CELEBRATION

Festival candles are kindled in the evening (the blessing is almost identical to that recited on Shabbat but ends with the phrase *"ner shel Yom Tov,"* "the holiday lights," on Rosh Hashanah and *"ner shel Yom HaKippurim,"* "the Yom Kippur lights," on Yom Kippur), *Kiddush* is recited on Rosh Hashanah, and the restrictions associated with Shabbat are observed during both holidays. Apples and honey (for a sweet year) and round challah (for a full year) are served on Rosh Hashanah; on Yom Kippur, it is customary to fast and to refrain from pleasurable activities. Many Jews attend evening and daytime services; the shofar is sounded during the Rosh Hashanah morning service, and services are held all day on Yom Kippur. Most synagogues offer children's services in the morning as well. Orthodox and Conservative Jews observe a second day of Rosh Hashanah.

IDEAS FOR CHILDREN

Talk about the concept of new beginnings for a new year: What are things your child liked and did not like about the past year? Which behaviors would he like to improve in the coming year? To whom should he say "I'm sorry" and why? (Your little one's self-awareness may astound you.) To celebrate Rosh Hashanah, bake a cake in honor of the "birthday of the world." Capitalize on the appeal of apples and honey: cook applesauce, make apple-print new year cards, taste-test different varieties and colors of apples, and learn about how bees make honey. To observe Yom Kippur, donate food to a local pantry or agency, and consider having your child forgo sweets for the day. Wear white to symbolize purity and forgiveness.

GOOD BOOKS FOR CHILDREN

Apples and Honey: A Rosh Hashanah Lift-the-Flap Book, by Joan Holub, illustrated by Cary Pillo-Lassen. Puffin Books.

Engineer Ari and the Rosh Hashanah Ride, by Deborah Bodin Cohen, illustrated by Shahar Kober. Kar-Ben Publishing.

Happy Birthday, World! A Rosh Hashanah Celebration, by Latifa Berry Kropf, illustrated by Lisa Carlson. Kar-Ben Publishing.

The Hardest Word: A Yom Kippur Story, by Jacqueline Jules, illustrated by
   Katherine Kahn. Kar-Ben Publishing.
The High Holy Days, written and illustrated by Camille Kress. URJ Press.
Sammy Spider's First Rosh Hashanah, by Sylvia A. Rouss, illustrated by
   Katherine Janus Kahn. Kar-Ben Publishing.
Sophie and the Shofar, by Fran Manushkin, illustrated by Rosalind Char-
   ney Kaye. URJ Press.
Sound the Shofar! A Story for Rosh Hashanah and Yom Kippur, by Leslie
   Kimmelman, illustrated by John Himmelman. HarperCollins.
The World's Birthday: A Rosh Hashanah Story, by Barbara Diamond Gol-
   din, illustrated by Jeanette Winter. Harcourt.
A Yom Kippur Think, by Miriam Feinberg, illustrated by Karen Ostrove.
   United Synagogue of Conservative Judaism Commission on Jewish
   Education.

Sukkot and Simchat Torah

An agricultural and historical holiday, Sukkot centers on the fall harvest
and the remembrance of the sukkot (temporary booths) in which our ancestors lived while wandering the desert after the Exodus. Just after Sukkot comes Simchat Torah—rejoicing in the Torah—the holiday during
which we complete the cycle of Torah readings and immediately begin
again with the story of Creation.

TRADITIONAL CELEBRATION

Sukkot lasts seven days—eight for Orthodox and Conservative Jews—
and the first and last days are especially sacred. Festival candles are kindled in the evening (the blessing ends with the phrase *"ner shel Yom Tov,"*
"the holiday lights"), *Kiddush* is recited, and the restrictions associated
with Shabbat are observed. A sukkah is constructed outdoors for welcoming guests, eating meals, and sometimes even for sleeping. A *lulav*
(branches of willow, palm, and myrtle) and *etrog* (citron fruit) are ritu-
ally waved. On Simchat Torah, family services are held and the Torah is
honored with special ceremony, including joyful singing, dancing, and
flag-waving.

IDEAS FOR CHILDREN

During Sukkot, discuss the importance of spending time outside, and how God cares for us by sustaining the natural world. Construct a real sukkah (it's easier than you might think—talk with your rabbi or look online for sukkah-building kits) or create a pretend one; make fruit-shaped decorations out of paper, or paint acorns, pinecones, and small gourds to hang from the ceiling of your home. Explore the wonders of God's natural world: Go on nature walks, craft nature collages or do leaf prints, learn about how food is harvested, and go apple picking. Have lots of picnics or try camping out in the backyard one night. On Simchat Torah, talk about the Torah as God's present to us—a gift of stories and rules for us to live by. What are some important rules your child knows? Make an edible Torah by spreading cream cheese, peanut butter, or honey on a flour tortilla, rolling it up with two big pretzel sticks, and tying it closed with a piece of licorice.

GOOD BOOKS FOR CHILDREN

It's Sukkah Time! by Latifa Berry Kropf, photographs by Tod Cohen. Kar-Ben Publishing.

K'tonton's Sukkot Adventure, by Sadie Rose Weilerstein, illustrated by Joe Boddy. Jewish Publication Society of America.

Leo and Blossom's Sukkah, written and illustrated by Jane Breskin Zalben. Henry Holt and Company.

Night Lights: A Sukkot Story, by Barbara Diamond Goldin, illustrated by Laura Elizabeth Sucher. URJ Press.

Sammy Spider's First Sukkot, by Sylvia A. Rouss, illustrated by Katherine Janus Kahn. Kar-Ben Publishing.

The Sukkah That I Built, by Rachel Groner Vorst, illustrated by Elizabeth Victor-Elsby. Hachai Publishing.

Tamar's Sukkah, by Ellie Gellman, illustrated by Shauna M. Kawasaki. Kar-Ben Publishing.

Chanukah

Lasting eight days, Chanukah commemorates the second-century B.C.E. victory of the Jewish people—led by the Maccabee brothers—over the

Syrian-Greek King Antiochus, who sought to prohibit the practice of Judaism. According to rabbinic legend, when the triumphant Maccabees went to rededicate the Jewish Temple, they found only a small bit of oil with which to kindle the holy lamp; God caused that oil miraculously to burn for eight days.

TRADITIONAL CELEBRATION

On each of the eight nights of Chanukah, candles are kindled in a special candelabra called a *chanukiyah*, or menorah. The blessing ends with the phrase *"ner shel Chanukah,"* "the Chanukah lights." *Dreidels*—tops marked with Hebrew letters symbolizing *"nes gadol haya sham,"* "a great miracle happened there"—are spun, and foods containing oil—including *latkes*, or potato pancakes, and *sufganiyot*, or jelly doughnuts—are prepared. Many families also exchange gifts and chocolate coins called *gelt*.

IDEAS FOR CHILDREN

For many children, Chanukah means gifts—and lots of them—as parents struggle to compete with Christmas's elaborate pageantry. But Chanukah has its own charms; try to de-emphasize the orgy of presents in favor of truly celebrating the holiday. Make each night of Chanukah a festive event; let your little one pick out the candles and help you light them, and sing and dance to Chanukah songs. (You can find great, easy-to-sing music online or at Judaica or synagogue gift shops. URJ Books and Music offers a wide selection of Jewish music. Visit URJBooksandMusic.com for details.) Play *dreidel* and eat the traditional foods—if you prefer not to bake your own, frozen *latkes* and *sufganiyot* from Dunkin Donuts will do nicely! Make handprint menorahs (your little one puts her hands in a stamp pad, then arranges her fingers so the thumbs are pressed together and the other eight fingers spread out in the shape of a menorah) and edible *dreidels* (poke a pretzel stick into a marshmallow, then use a dab of peanut butter to attach a Hershey kiss to the bottom of the marshmallow). Learn about the properties of oil by filling a clear plastic bottle with oil, water, and a few drops of food coloring, sealing it, and shaking it around. Talk about miracles, praying to only one God, and how we are never too small to stand up for what we believe in. If your child does receive gifts, consider opening them in the morning so that the promise of presents won't overshadow these other activities, and be sure to give *tzedakah* by donating money, food, clothing, or toys to the needy.

GOOD BOOKS FOR CHILDREN

The Chanukah Blessing, by Penninah Schram, illustrated by Jeffrey Allon. URJ Press.

Chanukah on the Prairie, by Burt Schuman, illustrated by Rosalind Charney Kaye. URJ Press.

The Chanukkah Guest, by Eric A. Kimmel, illustrated by Giora Carmi. Scholastic.

Hanukkah Lights, Hanukkah Nights, by Leslie Kimmelman, illustrated by John Himmelman. HarperFestival.

Happy Hanukkah, Biscuit! by Alyssa Satin Capucilli, illustrated by Pat Schories. HarperFestival.

Let There Be Lights! written and illustrated by Camille Kress. URJ Press.

One Night, One Hanukkah Night, written and illustrated by Ariel Backman. Jewish Publication Society of America.

The Runaway Latkes, by Leslie Kimmelman, illustrated by Paul Yalowitz. Albert Whitman & Company.

Sammy Spider's First Hanukkah, by Sylvia A. Rouss, illustrated by Katherine Janus Kahn. Kar-Ben Publishing.

Where's My Dreidel? A Hanukkah Lift-the-Flap Story, by Betty Schwartz, illustrated by Varda Livney. Little Simon.

TU BISH'VAT

Known as "the birthday of the trees," Tu BiSh'vat marks the new year for trees and the beginning of the spring season in Israel. The holiday's name denotes the date on which it falls; *tu* refers to the fifteenth day, and *biSh'vat* means "in Sh'vat"—so Tu BiSh'vat means simply "the fifteenth of [the Hebrew month] Sh'vat."

TRADITIONAL CELEBRATION

Trees are planted on Tu BiSh'vat, both in our own communities and in Israel through donations to the Jewish National Fund (jnf.org). Various fruits and nuts are tasted. Some Jews hold Tu BiSh'vat seders—festive meals with readings about and blessings for the natural world. In recent times, Tu BiSh'vat has become a focal point for Jewish conservation and recycling efforts.

IDEAS FOR CHILDREN

Talk about the beauty of nature and our role as its guardians and care-takers. Learn about the different seasons and how trees and plants "rest" during the winter and bloom in the spring. Go to a farmer's market or the grocery store and buy new fruits to sample. Write down your little one's reactions—how did he think they smelled, felt, and tasted?—and invite him to draw pictures of his favorites. Gather fallen leaves and sort them by color, shape, and texture. Let your little one get his hands dirty and plant—trees, flowers, herbs, anything! Grow grass by sprinkling grass seed on a damp sponge, or poke small holes in raw eggs, blow out the white and yolk, carefully slice off the top of the eggshells, have your child decorate the shells like faces, then place dirt and grass seed inside; in a week or so, your "eggheads" will sprout "hair"! Choose people to honor by planting trees in their name in Israel through the Jewish National Fund. Begin or expand your family's recycling program.

GOOD BOOKS FOR CHILDREN

The Giving Tree, written and illustrated by Shel Silverstein. HarperCollins.

Grandpa and Me on Tu B'Shevat, by Marji Gold-Vukson, illustrated by Leslie Evans. Kar-Ben Publishing.

It's Tu B'Shevat, by Edie Stoltz Zolkower, illustrated by Richard Johnson. Kar-Ben Publishing.

Solomon and the Trees, by Matt Biers-Ariel, illustrated by Esti Silverberg-Kiss. URJ Press.

Purim

Purim recalls the defeat of the wicked Haman, who plotted to kill the Jews of ancient Persia, at the hands of heroic Queen Esther and her uncle Mordechai. Recounted in the biblical Book of Esther, the story likely has little or no historical accuracy, but it has come to symbolize the Jewish people's escape from destruction and our eternal hope for redemption.

TRADITIONAL CELEBRATION

Purim is observed with much joy, merriment—and silliness. The *M'gillah*—the Book of Esther written on a special scroll—is read in the synagogue, and *gragers*, or noisemakers, are sounded whenever Haman's name is mentioned. Costumes are worn, humor—often irreverent—is injected into the service, and most congregations complement the festivities with a children's carnival. Triangular-shaped cookies called hamantaschen are eaten, and adults are actually encouraged to consume alcohol! *Sh'lach manot*—small gifts of food—are exchanged with friends, and *matanot l'evyomim*—portions to the poor, or *tzedakah*—are given.

IDEAS FOR CHILDREN

Because Purim so appeals to children, be sure to take your little one to synagogue for a *M'gillah* reading and carnival. (Even if you do not belong to a temple, most will be delighted to welcome your family.) Encourage your child to dress in costume, shake a *grager*, and just have a great time! You can also make your own *grager* by folding a paper plate in half, filling it with dry beans, sealing it closed, and decorating it with markers and stickers; bake hamantaschen (a yummy, easy recipe follows) to share with family and friends; and give *tzedakah*. Talk about the importance of being brave and smart, and standing up for who we are. Play "Esther, Mordechai, Haman," where you call out various names—including Esther, Mordechai, and Haman—and your child screams, yells, and stomps around whenever she hears "Haman." It will get your little one's wiggles out, and she will have a great time.

EASY HAMANTASCHEN RECIPE

In a chilled bowl, mix 3 sticks of butter with ¾ cup of sugar. Add 3 cups of flour, one at a time. Roll the dough into balls, then flatten the balls and pinch three corners to make triangles. Press chocolate chips into the center, and bake for 15 minutes at 325 degrees. Yum!

GOOD BOOKS FOR CHILDREN

It's Purim Time! by Latifa Berry Kropf, photographs by Tod Cohen. Kar-Ben Publishing.

The Mystery Bear: A Purim Story, by Leone Adelson, illustrated by Naomi Howland. Clarion Books.

Purim, written and illustrated by Carmen Bredeson. Children's Press.

Purim! written and illustrated by Camille Kress. URJ Press.

The Purim Costume, by Penninah Schram, illustrated by Tammi Keiser. URJ Press.

Sammy Spider's First Purim, by Sylvia A. Rouss, illustrated by Katherine Janus Kahn. Kar-Ben Publishing.

Passover

Passover celebrates one of the pivotal moments of Jewish history: the Exodus from Egypt and our redemption at the Red Sea. It also serves as an agricultural festival and marks the beginning of the barley harvest.

TRADITIONAL CELEBRATION

The centerpiece of Passover is the seder, a ritual meal of special foods and readings that dramatically recalls Israelite slavery and redemption. During the seven days of Passover (eight for Orthodox and Conservative Jews), no *hametz*—leavened food—is eaten; some Jews remove all traces of *hametz* from their homes. The first and last days of Passover are especially sacred; festival candles are kindled in the evening (the blessing ends with the phrase *"ner shel Yom Tov,"* "the holiday lights"), *Kiddush* is recited, and the restrictions associated with Shabbat are observed.

IDEAS FOR CHILDREN

Have your little one help you sort food according to what contains *hametz*, and take at least a few unopened boxes of *hametz* to a local pantry before Passover officially begins. Encourage your child to make or decorate ritual objects used during the seder: a matzah cover, a *Kiddush* cup, clay bowls for dipping, even a seder plate (some paint-your-own-ceramics shops have these available in early spring). Bake matzah by mixing flour, water, and a little salt, rolling out the dough and pricking it with a fork, and cooking it for about 10 minutes at 350 degrees, or prepare *charoset* by mixing finely chopped apples with wine, nuts, and cinnamon. (If your little one cannot have nuts, don't worry; nut-free *charoset* is plenty good, too!) Talk about the miracles God performs for us and the blessing of being free, and about our obligation to help people who are suffering. Of course, if it is at all possible, your child should participate in a seder, perhaps even assisting with the Four Questions; many synagogues hold seders that are open to the community, or your rabbi can advise you if you wish to try doing it yourself. (An extra treat for adults: After your little one is in bed, curl up with your spouse and a copy of the Song of Songs—a book of the Bible traditionally read during Passover. It is a collection of beautiful and erotic love poetry.)

GOOD BOOKS FOR CHILDREN

Company's Coming! A Passover Lift-the-Flap Book, by Joan Holub, illustrated by Renee Andriani-Williams. Puffin.

Hooray! It's Passover! by Leslie Kimmelman, illustrated by John Himmelman. HarperFestival.

A Little Girl Named Miriam, by Dina Rosenfeld, illustrated by Ilene Winn-Lederer. Hachai Publishing.

The Matzah Man: A Passover Story, written and illustrated by Naomi Howland. Clarion Books.

My First Passover Board Book, DK Publishing.

Sammy Spider's First Passover, by Sylvia A. Rouss, illustrated by Katherine Janus Kahn. Kar-Ben Publishing.

A Touch of Passover: A Touch and Feel Book, by Ari Sollish, illustrated by Boruch Becker. Merkos L'inyonei Chinuch.

A Tree Trunk Seder, written and illustrated by Camille Kress. URJ Press.

What I Like About Passover, written and illustrated by Varda Livney. Little Simon.

Where is the Afikomen? by Judyth Groner, pictures by Roz Schanzer. Kar-Ben Publishing.

Yom HaAtzma-ut and Shavuot

These joyful spring holidays mark the birth of the modern State of Israel and the giving of the Torah at Mount Sinai, respectively. While Yom HaAtzma-ut—literally, Independence Day—is obviously a new holiday and Shavuot an ancient agricultural and historical festival, both celebrate milestones of profound importance to our Jewish identity, and impart a sense of wonder and gratitude that we are witnesses to these amazing events.

TRADITIONAL CELEBRATION

Although some synagogues hold services for Yom HaAtzma-ut, it is primarily a secular holiday in the Diaspora, usually observed with community-sponsored festivities that focus on Israeli culture, food, music, dance, and the like. On the eve of Shavuot, study sessions on Jewish themes are often organized to recall the giving of the Torah; during the holiday, foods prepared with dairy are eaten, and the synagogue is decorated with fruits and flowers. Festival candles are kindled in the evening (the blessing ends with the phrase *"ner shel Yom Tov,"* "the holiday lights"), *Kiddush* is recited, and the restrictions associated with Shabbat are observed. Orthodox and Conservative Jews observe two days of Shavuot.

IDEAS FOR CHILDREN

Yom HaAtzma-ut is a wonderful opportunity to introduce your little one to the Land of Israel. Help him craft an Israeli flag by gluing two long strips of blue paper onto a white background, then adding a blue Star of David in the center. Parade around waving the flag and singing any Hebrew or Jewish songs he likes. Look at pictures of Israel in books or online; sample Israeli foods like hummus, falafel, and halva candy; and teach him basic Hebrew words like *"shalom"* (hello, goodbye, and peace), *"ema"* (mother), and *"abba"* (father). Bury coins and small treasures in a sandbox and let your child dig for "artifacts" just as people do in Israel. On Shavuot, have your little one close his eyes and imagine what it was like to receive the Torah; according to the Book of Exodus, Mount Sinai was aflame and quaking, and the thunderous call of the shofar echoed through the desert. (See Exodus 19:16–19 for more details.) Eat dairy foods like blintzes, kugel (a great and easy kugel recipe to use with your little one follows), and even ice cream. Decorate your home with fresh flowers, and bring gifts of fruit to those in need—as well as to friends and family.

GREAT KUGEL RECIPE

Cook an eight-ounce package of wide egg noodles and use them to line a greased 9-by-13-inch pan. In a blender, mix 1 cup of milk; ½ cup of butter or margarine; 8 ounces of cream cheese; 1 teaspoon of vanilla; ⅔ cup of sugar; and 4 eggs. Pour this mixture over the noodles, top with crushed cornflakes, sprinkle with cinnamon, and bake at 350 degrees for 45 minutes. Delicious!

GOOD BOOKS FOR CHILDREN

Agnon's Alef-Bet Poems, by S.Y. Agnon, illustrated by Arieh Zeldich. Jewish Publication Society of America.

The Child's Garden of Torah: A Read-Aloud Bedtime Bible, written and illustrated by Joel Lurie Grishaver. Torah Aura Productions.

Come, Let Us Be Joyful, by Fran Manushkin, illustrated by Rosalind Charney Kaye. URJ Press.

I Am a Torah, written and illustrated by Beily Paluch. Hachai Publishing.

A Mountain of Blintzes, by Barbara Diamond Goldin, illustrated by Anik McGrory. Gulliver Books.

Let's Visit Israel, by Judyth Saypol Groner, illustrated by Cheryl Nathan. Kar-Ben Publishing.

My Cousin Tamar Lives in Israel, by Michelle Shapiro Abraham, illustrated by Ann D. Koffsky. URJ Press.

Sammy Spider's First Trip to Israel, by Sylvia A. Rouss, illustrated by Katherine Janus Kahn. Kar-Ben Publishing.

APPENDIX C

Inspirational Prayers

Sh'ma

שְׁמַע יִשְׂרָאֵל יְהֹוָה אֱלֹהֵינוּ יְהֹוָה אֶחָד! בָּרוּךְ שֵׁם כְּבוֹד מַלְכוּתוֹ
לְעוֹלָם וָעֶד.

Sh'ma Yisrael: Adonai Eloheinu, Adonai echad!
Baruch shem k'vod malchuto l'olam va-ed!

Hear O Israel: The Eternal is our God, the Eternal God is One!
Blessed is God's glorious majesty forever and ever!

From The Bedtime *Sh'ma*: A Traditional Nighttime Prayer

You are blessed, Eternal One our God, Sovereign of the world, Who casts sleep upon my eyes and slumber upon my eyelids. May it be Your will, Eternal One, my God and the God of my mothers and fathers, that You lay me down to sleep in peace and raise me up in peace. May my dreams and thoughts and fears not confound me, and may my children be whole before You. You are blessed, Eternal One, Who illuminates the world with Your glory.

In the name of the Eternal One, the God of Israel: May Michael be at my right, Gabriel at my left, Uriel before me, and Raphael behind me. And above my head may rest the *Shechinah*, the Divine Presence of God.

The Priestly Benediction

Place your hands on your child's head, look into his or her eyes, and say:

יְבָרֶכְךָ יְיָ וְיִשְׁמְרֶךָ.
יָאֵר יְיָ פָּנָיו אֵלֶיךָ וִיחֻנֶּךָּ.
יִשָּׂא יְיָ פָּנָיו אֵלֶיךָ וְיָשֵׂם לְךָ שָׁלוֹם.

Y'varech'cha Adonai v'yishm'recha.
Ya-eir Adonai panav eilecha vichuneka.
Yisa Adonai panav eilecha v'yaseim l'cha shalom.

May God bless you and keep you.
May God shine God's face upon you and be good to you.
May God turn the Divine face toward you and give you peace.

Modeh (Modah) Ani: A Prayer Upon Awakening

מוֹדֶה (מוֹדָה) אֲנִי לְפָנֶיךָ, מֶלֶךְ חַי וְקַיָּם, שֶׁהֶחֱזַרְתָּ בִּי נִשְׁמָתִי
בְּחֶמְלָה. רַבָּה אֱמוּנָתֶךָ!

Modeh (modah) ani l'fanecha, Melech chai v'kayam, she-hechezarta bi
nishmati b'chemlah. Rabbah emunatecha!

I thank You, living and eternal God—with love, You have restored my soul within me. How great is Your compassion!

Nisim Kol Yom: Everyday Miracles

From the traditional morning blessings

בָּרוּךְ אַתָּה יְיָ, אֱלֹהֵינוּ מֶלֶךְ הָעוֹלָם, אֲשֶׁר נָתַן לַשֶּׂכְוִי בִינָה,
לְהַבְחִין בֵּין יוֹם וּבֵין לָיְלָה.

Baruch atah Adonai, Eloheinu Melech haolam, asher natan lasechvi vinah l'havchin bein yom uvein lailah.

You are blessed, Eternal One our God, Sovereign of the World, Who teaches us to distinguish between daylight and nightfall.

בָּרוּךְ אַתָּה יְיָ, אֱלֹהֵינוּ מֶלֶךְ הָעוֹלָם, שֶׁעָשַׂנִי יִשְׂרָאֵל.

Baruch atah Adonai, Eloheinu Melech haolam, she-asani Yisrael.

You are blessed, Eternal One our God, Sovereign of the World, Who makes me a Jew.

בָּרוּךְ אַתָּה יְיָ, אֱלֹהֵינוּ מֶלֶךְ הָעוֹלָם, שֶׁעָשַׂנִי בֶּן (בַּת) חוֹרִין.

Baruch atah Adonai, Eloheinu Melech haolam, she-asani ben (bat) chorin.

You are blessed, Eternal One our God, Sovereign of the World, Who makes me free.

בָּרוּךְ אַתָּה יְיָ, אֱלֹהֵינוּ מֶלֶךְ הָעוֹלָם, פּוֹקֵחַ עִוְרִים.

Baruch atah Adonai, Eloheinu Melech haolam, pokei-ach ivrim.

You are blessed, Eternal One our God, Sovereign of the World, Who opens the eyes of the blind.

בָּרוּךְ אַתָּה יְיָ, אֱלֹהֵינוּ מֶלֶךְ הָעוֹלָם, מַלְבִּישׁ עֲרֻמִּים.

Baruch atah Adonai, Eloheinu Melech haolam, malbish arumim.

You are blessed, Eternal One our God, Sovereign of the World, Who clothes the naked.

בָּרוּךְ אַתָּה יְיָ, אֱלֹהֵינוּ מֶלֶךְ הָעוֹלָם, מַתִּיר אֲסוּרִים.

Baruch atah Adonai, Eloheinu Melech haolam, matir asurim.

You are blessed, Eternal One our God, Sovereign of the World, Who frees the captive.

בָּרוּךְ אַתָּה יְיָ, אֱלֹהֵינוּ מֶלֶךְ הָעוֹלָם, זוֹקֵף כְּפוּפִים.

Baruch atah Adonai, Eloheinu Melech haolam, zokeif k'fufim.

You are blessed, Eternal One our God, Sovereign of the World, Who raises the oppressed.

בָּרוּךְ אַתָּה יְיָ, אֱלֹהֵינוּ מֶלֶךְ הָעוֹלָם, רוֹקַע הָאָרֶץ עַל הַמָּיִם.

Baruch atah Adonai, Eloheinu Melech haolam, roka haaretz al hamayim.

You are blessed, Eternal One our God, Sovereign of the World, Who sets the earth upon the waters.

בָּרוּךְ אַתָּה יְיָ, אֱלֹהֵינוּ מֶלֶךְ הָעוֹלָם, שֶׁעָשָׂה לִי כָּל צָרְכִּי.

Baruch atah Adonai, Eloheinu Melech haolam, she-asah li kol tzorki.

You are blessed, Eternal One our God, Sovereign of the World, Who fulfills all my needs.

בָּרוּךְ אַתָּה יְיָ, אֱלֹהֵינוּ מֶלֶךְ הָעוֹלָם, הַמֵּכִין מִצְעֲדֵי גָבֶר.

Baruch atah Adonai, Eloheinu Melech haolam, hameichin mitzadei gaver.

You are blessed, Eternal One our God, Sovereign of the World, Who makes firm my footsteps.

בָּרוּךְ אַתָּה יְיָ, אֱלֹהֵינוּ מֶלֶךְ הָעוֹלָם, אוֹזֵר יִשְׂרָאֵל בִּגְבוּרָה.

Baruch atah Adonai, Eloheinu Melech haolam, ozeir Yisrael big'vurah.

You are blessed, Eternal One our God, Sovereign of the World, Who grants courage to Israel.

בָּרוּךְ אַתָּה יְיָ, אֱלֹהֵינוּ מֶלֶךְ הָעוֹלָם, עוֹטֵר יִשְׂרָאֵל בְּתִפְאָרָה.

Baruch atah Adonai, Eloheinu Melech haolam, oteir Yisrael b'tifarah.

You are blessed, Eternal One our God, Sovereign of the World, Who crowns Israel with glory.

בָּרוּךְ אַתָּה יְיָ, אֱלֹהֵינוּ מֶלֶךְ הָעוֹלָם, הַנּוֹתֵן לַיָּעֵף כֹּחַ.

Baruch atah Adonai, Eloheinu Melech haolam, hanotein laya-eif ko-ach.

You are blessed, Eternal One our God, Sovereign of the World, Who strengthens the weary.

Prayers for Special Occasions

SHEHECHEYANU: FOR SPECIAL MOMENTS

בָּרוּךְ אַתָּה יְיָ, אֱלֹהֵינוּ מֶלֶךְ הָעוֹלָם, שֶׁהֶחֱיָנוּ וְקִיְּמָנוּ וְהִגִּיעָנוּ
לַזְּמַן הַזֶּה.

Baruch atah Adonai, Eloheinu Melech haolam, shehecheyanu v'kiy'manu v'higianu laz'man hazeh.

You are blessed, Eternal One our God, Sovereign of the world, Who has kept us in life, sustained us, and brought us to this moment.

FOR PUTTING ON NEW CLOTHES

בָּרוּךְ אַתָּה יְיָ, אֱלֹהֵינוּ מֶלֶךְ הָעוֹלָם, מַלְבִּישׁ עֲרֻמִּים.

Baruch atah Adonai, Eloheinu Melech haolam, malbish arumim.

You are blessed, Eternal One our God, Sovereign of the World, Who clothes the naked.

DURING A THUNDERSTORM

בָּרוּךְ אַתָּה יְיָ, אֱלֹהֵינוּ מֶלֶךְ הָעוֹלָם, שֶׁכֹּחוֹ וּגְבוּרָתוֹ מָלֵא עוֹלָם.

Baruch atah Adonai, Eloheinu Melech haolam, shekocho ug'vurato malei olam.

You are blessed, Eternal One our God, Sovereign of the World, Whose strength and might fill the world.

FOR SEEING A RAINBOW

בָּרוּךְ אַתָּה יְיָ, אֱלֹהֵינוּ מֶלֶךְ הָעוֹלָם, זוֹכֵר הַבְּרִית, וְנֶאֱמָן
בִּבְרִיתוֹ, וְקַיָּם בְּמַאֲמָרוֹ.

Baruch atah Adonai, Eloheinu Melech haolam, zocheir habrit v'ne-eman bivrito v'kayam b'ma-amaro.

You are blessed, Eternal One our God, Sovereign of the World, Who remembers the covenant and is faithful in keeping promises.

FOR SEEING A WISE PERSON

בָּרוּךְ אַתָּה יְיָ, אֱלֹהֵינוּ מֶלֶךְ הָעוֹלָם, שֶׁנָּתַן מֵחָכְמָתוֹ לְבָשָׂר וָדָם.

Baruch atah Adonai, Eloheinu Melech haolam, shenatan meichochmato le'vasar vadam.

You are blessed, Eternal One our God, Sovereign of the World, Who shares divine wisdom with those of flesh and blood.

FOR SEEING A BEAUTIFUL PERSON, ANIMAL, OR PLANT

בָּרוּךְ אַתָּה יְיָ, אֱלֹהֵינוּ מֶלֶךְ הָעוֹלָם, שֶׁכָּכָה לוֹ בְּעוֹלָמוֹ.

Baruch atah Adonai, Eloheinu Melech haolam, shekacha lo b'olamo.

You are blessed, Eternal One our God, Sovereign of the World, Who holds wonders in Your world.

FOR SEEING THE OCEAN, MOUNTAINS, VALLEYS, RIVERS, AND WILDERNESS

בָּרוּךְ אַתָּה יְיָ, אֱלֹהֵינוּ מֶלֶךְ הָעוֹלָם, עוֹשֶׂה מַעֲשֵׂה בְרֵאשִׁית.

Baruch atah Adonai, Eloheinu Melech haolam, oseh maaseh v'reishit.

You are blessed, Eternal One our God, Sovereign of the World, Maker of the works of creation.

Blessings for Eating

HAMOTZI, RECITED BEFORE MEALS:

בָּרוּךְ אַתָּה יְיָ, אֱלֹהֵינוּ מֶלֶךְ הָעוֹלָם, הַמּוֹצִיא לֶחֶם מִן הָאָרֶץ.

Baruch atah Adonai, Eloheinu Melech haolam, hamotzi lechem min haaretz.

You are blessed, Eternal One our God, Sovereign of the world, Who brings forth bread from the earth.

BIRKAT HAMAZON, THE BLESSING FOR SUSTENANCE, RECITED AFTER MEALS:

בָּרוּךְ אַתָּה יְיָ, אֱלֹהֵינוּ מֶלֶךְ הָעוֹלָם, הַזָּן אֶת־הָעוֹלָם כֻּלּוֹ בְּטוּבוֹ,
בְּחֵן בְּחֶסֶד וּבְרַחֲמִים. הוּא נוֹתֵן לֶחֶם לְכָל־בָּשָׂר, כִּי לְעוֹלָם חַסְדּוֹ!
וּבְטוּבוֹ הַגָּדוֹל תָּמִיד לֹא חָסַר לָנוּ, וְאַל יֶחְסַר לָנוּ מָזוֹן לְעוֹלָם
וָעֶד. בַּעֲבוּר שְׁמוֹ הַגָּדוֹל, כִּי הוּא אֵל זָן וּמְפַרְנֵס לַכֹּל, וּמֵטִיב לַכֹּל,
וּמֵכִין מָזוֹן לְכָל בְּרִיּוֹתָיו אֲשֶׁר בָּרָא. בָּרוּךְ אַתָּה יְיָ, הַזָּן אֶת־הַכֹּל.

*Baruch atah Adonai, Eloheinu Melech haolam, hazan et haolam ḳulo
b'tuvo—b'chein, b'chesed uv'rachamim. Hu notein lechem l'chol basar,
ḳi l'olam chasdo! Uv'tuvo hagadol tamid lo chasar lanu, v'al yechsar lanu
mazon l'olam va-ed. Baavur sh'mo hagadol, ḳi hu El zan um'farneis laḳol,
u'meitiv laḳol u'meichin mazon l'chol b'riyotav asher bara. Baruch atah
Adonai, hazan et haḳol.*

You are blessed, Eternal One our God, Sovereign of the World, Who
sustains the world—all of it—with Your goodness, with grace and
kindness and compassion. God grants food to all flesh, for God's kindness is everlasting! For the sake of God's greatness, God will never let
us want for sustenance. In God's great name, God feeds and sustains
us all, caring for all the divine Creation. You are blessed, Eternal One,
Who gives food to all.

Acknowledgments

The ancient sage Rabbi Chanina confessed, "I have learned much from my teachers and more from my colleagues—but most of all I have learned from my students."[1] I have learned much from authors, experts, teachers, and pediatricians, and more from other parents—but most of all I have learned from our three wonderful children: Moses Aaron, Leo Baeck, and Eden Rose. I thank God every day for the privilege of being your mother, and I love you with all my heart.

I am blessed to know so many special people whose support and expertise have made this book possible. Thank you to Rabbi Samuel Karff, Dr. Edward Goldman, and Dr. Richard Sarason, whose inspired teaching and remarkable kindness taught me to love midrash; Dr. Stephen Bolline and Juli Villareal—pediatrician and nurse extraordinaire; Elida Villatoro; Kat Heard and Clare Carter; and the incomparable and amazing Barbie Freedman and Suzanne Shanoff. I am also grateful for the insight of Dr. Alan Cooper and Dr. Stanley Tsigounis; the generous assistance of the staff of Klau Library at Hebrew Union College-Jewish Institute of Religion's Cincinnati and New York campuses; and the encouragement and expertise of Michael Goldberg, Rabbi Hara Person, Lori Lesser, Michelle Shapiro Abraham, Laurie Buchsbaum, and Casey Wolfer. Finally, thank you to the faculty of four extraordinary institutions: The Shlenker

---

[1] *Taanit* 7a.

School of Houston, Texas, and the Temple Emanu-El Preschool, Goldie Feldman Academy, and Forty Carrots Family Center of Sarasota, Florida. You have enriched and nurtured my children—and me!—and I am most appreciative.

Our tradition teaches, "Either companionship or death"[2]—and I thank God for those wonderful people in my life who have sustained me by choosing the former. I am proud to stand among the fabulous Farfel women—Carol, Linda, Cheryl, Susan, Julie, Laurie, Lori, and Caroline—and their equally fabulous spouses—Barry, Herb, Haran, Syd, Robert, Larry, Daniel, and Brian—and offer them my awestruck thanks for being the incredible family they are—and for always making sure we never left their homes hungry. More unending love and gratitude to Judy and Al Glickman, Cherie Azad, Kelly Hess, and especially and always Emily Page. To my grandmother Pearl Rose and my parents, Helen and Larry Rose—I could say thank you every minute for the rest of my life, but that wouldn't begin to cover it. And finally, to Brenner—you are my beloved, and you are my friend. I love you more than I can say.

---

[2]*Taanit* 23a, in Klagsbrun, 42.

Bibliography

Abrams, Rabbi Judith Z. and Dr. Steven A. *Jewish Parenting: Rabbinic Insights*. Northvale, NJ: Jason Aronson, 1994.

American Baby Magazine, various issues.

Baby Talk Magazine, various issues.

Bell, Roselyn, editor. *The Hadassah Magazine Jewish Parenting Book*. New York: The Free Press, 1989.

Bettelheim, Bruno. *A Good Enough Parent*. New York: Vintage, 1987.

Bialik, H.N. and Y.H. Ravnitzky, eds. *The Book of Legends*, translated by William G. Braude. New York: Schocken Books, 1992.

Bronstein, Herbert, ed. *A Passover Haggadah: The New Union Haggadah, Second Revised Edition*. New York: Central Conference of American Rabbis and Penguin Books, 1982.

Canter, Lee and Marlene. *Assertive Discipline*. Santa Monica, CA: Lee Canter and Associates, 1992.

Canter, Lee and Marlene. *Assertive Discipline for Parents: Revised Edition*. Santa Monica, CA: Canter and Associates, 1985.

Child Magazine, various issues.

Cohen, Debra Nussbaum. *Celebrating Your New Jewish Daughter: Creating Jewish Ways to Welcome Baby Girls into the Covenant*. Woodstock, VT: Jewish Lights Publishing, 2001.

Crittenden, Ann. *The Price of Motherhood: Why the Most Important Job in the World Is Still the Least Valued*. New York: Henry Holt and Company, 2001.

Danby, Herbert, D.D., translator. *The Mishnah*. New York: Oxford University Press, 1933.

Donin, Rabbi Hayim Halevy. *To Be a Jew: A Guide to Jewish Observance in Contemporary Life*. New York: Basic Books, 1972.

Douglas, Susan J. and Meredith W. Michaels. *The Mommy Myth: The Idealization of Motherhood and How It Has Undermined Women*. New York: The Free Press, 2004.

Eisenberg, Arlene, Heidi E. Murkoff, and Sandee E. Hathaway, B.S.N. *What to Expect: The Toddler Years*. New York: Workman Publishing, 1994.

Elkind, David. *Miseducation: Preschoolers at Risk*. New York: Alfred A. Knopf, 1987.

Encyclopedia Judaica. Jerusalem: Keter Publishing House, 1971.

Epstein, I., ed. *The Babylonian Talmud*. London: The Soncino Press, 1960.

Epstein, Jane Geller. *The Jewish Working Parent*. New York: United Synagogue of Conservative Judaism Commission on Jewish Education, 1988.

Freedman, H. and Maurice Simon, eds. *The Midrash Rabbah*. London: The Soncino Press, 1977.

Fuchs-Kreimer, Nancy. *Parenting as a Spiritual Journey*. Woodstock, VT: Jewish Lights Publishing, 1996.

Goodman, Robert. *A Teacher's Guide to the Jewish Holidays*. Denver: A.R.E. Publishing, 1983.

Hoffner, Rabbi Naftali, compiler. *Guide to Blessings*. New York: NCSY, 1986.

Hogg, Tracy, with Melinda Blau. *Secrets of the Baby Whisperer for Toddlers*. New York: Ballantine Books, 2002.

Iovine, Vicki. *The Girlfriends' Guide to Toddlers*. New York: Perigee, 1999.

Isaacs, Ronald H. *Raising a Jewish Child: Early Years*. New York: United Synagogue of Conservative Judaism Commission on Jewish Education, 2000.

The Jerusalem Bible. Jerusalem: Koren Publishers, 1992.

Kindlon, Dan, Ph.D. *Too Much of a Good Thing: Raising Children of Character in an Indulgent Age*. New York: Hyperion, 2001.

Klagsbrun, Francine. *Voices of Wisdom: Jewish Ideals and Ethics for Everyday Living*. New York: Jonathan David Publishers, 1986.

Krueger, Anne. *Parenting Guide to Your Baby's First Year*. New York: Ballantine Books, 1999.

Levi, Miriam. *Effective Jewish Parenting*. New York/Jerusalem: Feldheim Publishers, 1986.

Mellor, Christie. *The Three-Martini Playdate: A Practical Guide to Happy Parenting*. San Francisco: Chronicle Books, 2004.

Mogel, Wendy, Ph.D. *The Blessing of a Skinned Knee: Using Jewish Teachings to Raise Self-Reliant Children*. New York: Penguin Compass, 2001.

Parenting Magazine, various issues.

Parents Magazine, various issues.

Radcliffe, Sarah Chana. *The Delicate Balance*. Southfield, MI: Targum Press, 1989.

Radcliffe, Sarah Chana. *Raise Your Kids Without Raising Your Voice*. Toronto: Collins, 2006.

Rosman, Steven M. *Jewish Parenting Wisdom*. Northvale, NJ: Jason Aronson, 1997.

Saltsman, Rosally. *Parenting by the Book*. Southfield, MI: Targum Press, 2003.

Shelov, Steven P., M.D., F.A.A.P., editor-in-chief. *Caring For Your Baby and Young Child: Birth to Age 5*. New York: Bantam Books, 2004.

Siegel, Danny, ed. *Where Heaven and Earth Touch*. Pittsboro, NC: The Town House Press, 1996.

Spock, Benjamin, M.D. and Steven J. Parker, M.D. *Dr. Spock's Baby and Child Care, Seventh Edition*. New York: Pocket Books, 1998.

Steiner, Leslie Morgan, ed. *Mommy Wars: Stay-at-Home and Career Moms Face Off on Their Choices, Their Lives, Their Families*. New York: Random House, 2006.

Stern, Chaim, ed. *Gates of Prayer: The New Union Prayerbook.* New York: Central Conference of American Rabbis, 1975.

Stern, Chaim, ed. *Gates of Repentance: The New Union Prayerbook for the Days of Awe.* New York: Central Conference of American Rabbis, 1984.

Stern, Chaim, ed. *On the Doorposts of Your House.* New York: Central Conference of American Rabbis, 1994.

Strassfeld, Sharon and Kathy Green. *The Jewish Family Book: A Creative Approach to Raising Kids.* Toronto: Bantam Books, 1981.

Tanakh: The Holy Scriptures. Philadelphia: The Jewish Publication Society of America, 1985.

Telushkin, Rabbi Joseph. *Jewish Humor: What the Best Jewish Jokes Say About the Jews.* New York: William Morrow and Company, 1992.

Telushkin, Rabbi Joseph. *Jewish Wisdom: Ethical, Spiritual, and Historical Lessons from the Great Works and Thinkers.* New York: William Morrow and Company, 1994.

Twerski, Abraham J. *Positive Parenting.* Brooklyn, NY: Mesorah Publications, 1996.

Warner, Judith. *Perfect Madness: Motherhood in the Age of Anxiety.* New York: Riverhead Books, 2005.

Wikler, Meir. *Partners with Hashem.* Brooklyn, NY: Mesorah Publications, 2000.